Dorothea Fischer-Hornung

EmBODYing Liberation

Brooke House College

513989

FORECAAST

(Forum for European Contributions
to African American Studies)

Volume 4

LIT

Dorothea Fischer-Hornung, Alison D. Goeller (eds.)

EmBODYing Liberation

The Black Body in American Dance

LIT

Cover: "To Midnight Nan at Leroy's"
    Aaron Douglas, 1928
        Courtesy of the National Urban League ©

LOCATION: LRC
COLLECTION: CAN
CLASS MARK: 792.8088MB
BARCODE No: 513989
DATE: 26|11|03

Die Deutsche Bibliothek – CIP-Einheitsaufnahme

EmBODYing Liberation : The Black Body in American Dance /
Dorothea Fischer-Hornung, Alison D. Goeller (eds.). – Hamburg : LIT, 2001
    (FORECAAST ; 4.)
    ISBN 3-8258-4473-0

© LIT VERLAG Münster – Hamburg – London
    Grindelberg 15a 20144 Hamburg Tel. 040 - 44 64 46 Fax 040 - 44 14 22

Distributed in North America by:

Transaction Publishers
New Brunswick (U.S.A.) and London (U.K.)

Transaction Publishers
Rutgers University
35 Berrue Circle
Piscataway, NJ 08854

Tel.: (732) 445 - 2280
Fax: (732) 445 - 3138
for orders (U. S. only):
toll free (888) 999 - 6778

Contents

List of Illustrations

Acknowledgments

The papers gathered in this volume are the result of a panel on African American dance held in Muenster, Germany, in the spring of 1999, as part of the Collegium for African American Research (CAAR) Conference, *Black Liberation in the Americas*. Those of us who took part in the workshop – Christy Adair, Ramsay Burt, Dorothea Fischer-Hornung, Alison D. Goeller, and Dorota Janowska,– agreed that there was still much work to be done. And so, after the conference, we set out to do it.

Our thanks go to the participants of the conference, whose enthusiasm and expertise provided the initial spark, as well as to Maria Dietrich, CAAR's president, who encouraged us to collect our panel's papers and to solicit additional contributors. Thanks also go to Frank Funicello, who tirelessly read our manuscript and offered his own valuable editorial insights; Kurt Fischer, whose expertise in layout and design we could not have done without; and Uwe Jacobs, of the Festspielhaus Baden-Baden for arranging an interview with Judith Jamison and dancers of the Alvin Ailey American Dance Theater. Wendy Perron helped procure the rights to photos used in this volume and Isaac Julien agreed to share his insights into the making of his film *Three*. Special acknowledgment goes to Brenda Dixon Gottschild, who read our manuscript with both a dancer's eye and a scholar's perception, and Thomas DeFrantz, who enthusiastically offered us encouragement and advice. We believe the current volume reflects the variety and richness of the scholarship in the field of the black dancing body.

Dorothea Fischer-Hornung and Alison D. Goeller
Heidelberg, December 2000

Foreword: Black Bodies Dancing Black Culture – Black Atlantic Transformations

Thomas F. DeFrantz

More and more often, we are invited to read dance history that pays particular attention to cultural and political contexts for its production. This shift in critical writing, buoyed by the increase in performance studies and cultural studies perspectives, allows us to consider what particular dances *mean*, across time periods and geographies, for their dancers and audiences. More than this, the widening of critical lenses to locate African diaspora dance as a constellation of expressive practices and political circumstances leads us back – emphatically – to the body in motion. Increasingly, we are asked to consider dancing black bodies as the agents of social change, as case studies of identities in formation, and as avatars of ethnically-inflected artistic expression.

But do dancing black bodies always dance black? For many African American cultural historians, the critical category of "black dance" encompasses only social dance. In the realm of the social, the dancing bodies and their audiences merge. We must begin inside the circle. Frantz Fanon writes:

> The circle of the dance is a permissive circle: it protects and permits.... [Dance] may be deciphered, as in an open book, [as] the huge effort of a community to exorcise itself, to liberate itself, to explain itself. There are no limits – inside the circle. (57)[1]

But what happens outside of the circular realm of the social? How does concert dance created and performed by African American artists fall into and outside of the circle that protects and permits?

By invoking Fanon, I make a gesture towards blackness as an existential and corporeal reality. I want to claim the existence of "core black culture" that embraces the performative idioms of black expressive culture – music, oratory, fashion, game-playing, dance. All of these are generated within the circle that permits and protects. But all of them can also be accessed by cultural outsiders positioned well beyond the circle that permits and protects. More importantly, elements of black dance can be recognized and documented when the generative circle of the dance is opened to outside viewers.

Consider Bill "Bojangles" Robinson in the 1943 film *Stormy Weather*. Robinson's dance we recognize unequivocally as black dance. He speaks through rhythm in the so-called vernacular – a designation underscored in this film as a

---

[1] Frantz Fanon, *The Wretched of the Earth*. Trans. by Constance Farrington. New York: Grove Press, 1963.

longstanding tradition of stylized social dances which can be rearranged for the stage of popular entertainments. In the film, Robinson plays a man who aspires to be a professional dancer and spends his young adult life teaching himself variations on familiar steps until he is able, in true Hollywood ending fashion, to land a spot in a glamorous stage production. A significant sequence in the film, early in Robinson's ascent toward professionalization, emphasizes his experimentation with social dance idioms within a protective circle of musicians in the belly of a boat. Robinson tests his tapped social dance inventions in a smooth sequence of seemingly inevitable rhythmic ideas, coughing accentuations of cross-rhythms and subtle, ironic turns of rhythmic phrase that consolidate the underlying duple-meter form of the musical accompaniment. The irony of calling Robinson's artistry – or the idiom that he engages here – "vernacular" can't be lost on us as viewers; we marvel at his ability to transform open silences into active rhythmic breaks, and, with one toe, to describe circles containing the potency of temporal disruption and control on the deck of the ship. Surely he achieves transcendent mastery even here within the film's narrative of the naturalized, self-taught black dance. But if this is vernacular dance, we should each be able to reproduce it, or at least approach it. Are there any volunteers?

There is danger in talking about "black dance," even within the ubiquitous quotation marks that often surround "race." How willing are we to compress elaborate cultural practices into a neat package? Can we theorize something called "black identity" that contributes to articulations of "black dance?" Like British cultural theorist Paul Gilroy, I think that we have to. Gilroy writes:

> Black identity is not simply a social and political category to be used or abandoned according to the extent to which the rhetoric that supports and legitimizes it is persuasive or institutionally powerful ... it is lived as a coherent (if not always stable) experiential sense of self. Though it is often felt to be natural and spontaneous, it remains the outcome of practical activity: language, gesture, bodily significations, desires. (1993a, 102) [2]

My body understands how to be inside and a part of the circle that protects and permits. The practical activity of my dance – my gesture, my words, and what I mean to tell you by my stance – all contribute to how I construct my own black identity. It is not a singular construction; it has no proscriptive limits of gender, sexuality, or caste. My life as a black person is coherent and always changing. My experience follows Gilroy in its complexity; I am aware that "the fundamental, time-worn assumptions of homogenous and unchanging black communities whose political and economic interests were readily knowable and

---

[2]   Paul Gilroy, *The Black Atlantic: Modernity and Double Consciousness*. Cambridge: Harvard UP, 1993a.

easily transferred from everyday life into their expressive cultures has ... proved to be a fantasy" (1993b, 1).[3]

But this raises another series of questions. Does the black body, publicly displayed, automatically become a privileged "racial" sign? Black people dance inside the circle. The circle permits and protects. Black dance emerges inside the circle. The circle does not distinguish between private and public. Where, then, does this public display occur?

We might do well to consider a counternarrative of public spaces as "white spaces." I contend that a public space – at least in terms of concert dance – is a white space, a space of production and consumption, a modernist space, a fetishized space, a Europeanist space. A display of the black body in any of these spaces confers a responsibility onto the artist, who assumes "custodianship of the racial group's most intimate self-identity. The black body makes explicit the hidden links between blacks and helps to ground an oppositional aesthetic constituted around our phenotypical difference from 'white' ideals of beauty and a concept of the body in motion which is the residue of our African cultures" (Gilroy 1993b, 246). Significantly, this public space is outside the circle that protects and permits. Think back to Robinson and his quick-footed time step: what would he have said had there not been a militia of white crew members, producers, scriptwriters, songwriters, casting agents, studio chiefs and intended audiences tearing open the circle where he danced? Would he have smiled so aggressively to those omnipresent, but invisible, white bodies? Might he have allowed us to *feel* what his dance meant, beyond the surface effect of what his body was permitted to do?

In many circumstances, African American dancers break open the circle that protects and permits. Gilroy writes of contemporary black social dance: "Instead of taking our places in the circle of the dance where subordination was ambivalently enacted, transcended, and transformed ... we are invited to consume particularity just like any other commodity. The ring shout gives way to polite applause" (1997, 22).[4] Here, the performer no longer dissolves into the crowd, thereby enacting a relationship of black identity in antiphonal call and response forms. The dancer offers stylized movements as objects to be casually consumed by immobile spectators.

But what of our concert dancer, already removed from the realm of the social by virtue of her interest in focused aesthetic principals adopted from Western ideals? I offer that she might, by necessity, align herself with the African diaspora. Here, she will take comfort in the multitudes similarly disenfranchised and deposited in the New and Old Worlds without recourse to a "real"

---

3   Paul Gilroy, *Small Acts: Thoughts on the Politics of Black Cultures*. London: Serpent's Tail, 1993b.
4   Paul Gilroy, "Exer(or)cising Power: Black Bodies in the Black Public Sphere." *Dance In The City*. Ed. Helen Thomas. New York: St. Martin's P, 1997. 21–34.

homeland. The African diaspora is a utopia; an "eruption of space into the linear temporal order of modern black politics which enforces the obligation that space and time must be considered relationally" (Gilroy 1993a, 198). It is a tool for survival. The diaspora closes our circle for the dance across time and space. Through it, we black dancers allow ourselves to collaborate whether we understand each other or not.

The diaspora enlivens us and simultaneously reminds us to mourn. Its ubiquity constantly turns us towards death and "points to the ways in which black cultural forms have hosted and even cultivated a dynamic rapport with the presence of death and suffering" (Gilroy 1993a, 198). Because there is no "real" Africa in diaspora, we gain access to inexhaustible storehouses of pain, suffering, expressions of loss, exile, and eternal journeying. Gilroy discusses music, but the same is true for dance; this rapport with death "serves a mnemonic function: directing the consciousness of the group back to significant, nodal points in its common history and its social memory" (1993a, 198). The Black Atlantic actually encodes this diasporic longing into a historical moment: born of the rupture of the Middle Passage, the Black Atlantic is a "non-traditional tradition, an irreducibly modern, ex-centric, unstable, and asymmetrical cultural ensemble that cannot be apprehended through the manichean logic of binary coding" (Gilroy 1993a, 198). We mourn what can never really be – the diaspora, or its undoing through repatriation – and we dance inside the circle to mourn our loss. The circle permits and protects our memory of loss.

The Black Atlantic means to allow us a common dialectic as Africans in diaspora. According to Gilroy and others, antiphony, or call and response, is the principal formal feature of its artistic practices and expressive cultures. Antiphony works best in physical intimacy, within a circle where all can see the other dancers across the way.

Moving into the circle, I ask: where is the Black Atlantic located in concert dance gesture? Where is it? Richard Wright locates its expression in the diasporic tradition of bitterness, while Gilroy calls this the condition of "being in pain" (1993a, 203). Either articulation suggests that we will recognize the Black Atlantic in concert dance through a pervasive dissatisfaction with existing modes of expression; a need and desire to remake concert dance – that is, dance of the open circle – in some unique idiom or perverse restructuring of what came before. If the circle that permits and protects must be opened, it will deny its audience's expectations of comfort; it will force you to mourn, or shout, or become enraged so that you might enter into dialogue with its bitter tongue; so that you might somehow close the circle that permits and protects. The Black Atlantic gesture in concert dance intends to force its audience to presence, that we might see each other across the footlights.

Consider a concert dance of the Black Atlantic; Donald Byrd's newly-minted *In A Different Light: Duke Ellington*, created in 1999. In the first act of the three-part piece, titled "A Gentle Prelude," Byrd takes us outside the familiar, permissive circle of black dance with a work decidedly grounded on the proscenium stage. Still, I recognize his bitter choreographic tongue. The dance encodes antiphony as a choreographic technique: a slow, extended lean is answered by a fast, erect stride across the stage; a lyrical break in Ellington's piano score is undercut by an abrupt jab of an arm into the air. And there is more revisioning on a conceptual level: clearly, the work is a meditation on George Balanchine's *Serenade* of 1934, danced here by modern dancers to an assembled score by Ellington. As a whole, the work trades on an excess of virtuosic display, an excess of rhythmic progressions housed within an overarching abstract framework that gathers momentum as it goes along. In this dance, the audience is made aware of what Gilroy calls the "ethics of antiphony" (1993a, 207) – portrayed here as a cresting and falling tension between the lyrical piano score and the weighty, percussive movements of Byrd's choreography.

But this dance offers an obviously complex relationship to the Black Atlantic and longed-for, diasporic circle of the dance. Consider another contemporary work – choreographer Ronald K. Brown's *Grace*, made for the Alvin Ailey American Dance Theater, also in 1999. This work is much easier to discuss in terms of its relation to the Black Atlantic paradigm. I sense the "get-down" qualities of the movement and its performance; the celebratory aspects of its house music score; the depiction of black machismo in the line of shirtless men whose virility and steamy cool force me to cheer against all my heteronormative tendencies. When I saw the entire dance in performance twice in its first season, I understood more about its construction: its arching sacred dimension contained by its musical frame, the Duke Ellington spiritual "Come Sunday"; its deployment of black bodies as privileged racial signs able to fully explore the shifting rhythmic changes of the recorded score; its choreographic recuperation of neo-African idioms in its movement lexicon that grant the work an aura of authenticity. As a friend told me, the dancing black bodies perform movements that "suit them to a 'T'." Here, in the evening at a proscenium theater, they remind me of a night somewhere else, in a night club: of dances that explicitly express desire and regret, desire for intimacy with another and regret for the lack of true cultural coherency.

In its entirety, *Grace* explores sexuality and its discursive limits; the loss and recovery of spirituality, described here by a devotional leader and her efforts to assemble her charges; and, of course, a certain kind of kinetic bitterness in several solo passages of jagged, inward-focused rhythmic passages. The half-hour work begins with a soloist clad in white who enters the central performance space from an offstage sanctuary; she consecrates the stage for dancing by the group clad mostly in red; after a night on the town – or in the clubs, if you will – the dancers all change to white clothing and follow the devotional leader into the sanctuary suggested at the back of the stage space.

In telling a story of the black church, choreographer Brown evokes the memory of slavery which, ultimately, gave rise to the black church. He positions the dance firmly within a modernist tradition born of the Middle Passage and the gross cultural ruptures that slavery enacted. The dance becomes black dance, within the protective and permissive circle, not only in its outward, kinetic features, but in its opaque narrative of church practice; in its final tableau of diasporic wandering as the dancers amble away from the audience singly, but as a group, towards an offstage place of worship. Moreover, Brown's work references the mythologized "black vernacular" in its use of house music, club stance, and spontaneous-seeming bursts of dynamic physical energy.

This takes us back to vernacular dance and the problem of conflating the everyday gesture with the extraordinary. Concert dance is never vernacular; dance that is prepared can only make reference to dance that emerges within the closed black space. So what of our circle? Is it exclusive to black dancers in "core black cultural spaces?" Can "black dance" stretch to accommodate work by white choreographers? Certainly. Its aesthetic principles can be learned, and then the protective circle can form around a new, hybrid dance. We certainly see this in white hip hop, in cheerleading, in some concert dance choreography by choreographers who do not claim African ancestry. But this reformation often inspires failures in readings, as audiences, dancers, and choreographers don't necessarily understand their relationship to the circle. The circle protects and permits. When it is opened, we are no longer protected, although we may be permitted. Gilroy reminds us that "the globalization of vernacular forms means that our understanding of antiphony will have to change. The calls and responses no longer converge in the tidy patterns of secret, ethnically encoded dialogue" (1993a, 110).

But this change in locality that Gilroy predicts needn't be conceived as a loss; in terms of dance scholarship, it may most definitely be a gain. The migration of African diaspora dance forms from the closed circles of social spaces to the open circle of the concert stage allows us an enormous opportunity to document performance and its vital impact on culture in re/formation. The transformations of African-derived movements through the Middle Passage, and their emergence in the Americas and Europe as elements of concert dance, hold enormous significance for scholars working to construct histories of the body in motion. These particular histories – of black bodies dancing black – form the body, the corporeal essence, of the essays assembled in this remarkable volume.

Thomas F. DeFrantz
New York, December 2000

Introduction

Black Bodies in American Dance: Reflections on Aesthetics, Representations, and the Public Performance

Alison Goeller, Dorothea Fischer-Hornung and Dorota Janowska

> Mll. Taglioni reminded you of cool and shaded valleys, where a white vision
> suddenly emerges from the bark of an oak to greet the eyes of a young, sur-
> prised, and blushing shepherd; she resembles unmistakably those fairies of
> Scotland of whom Walter Scott speaks, who roam in the moonlight near the
> mysterious fountain, with a necklace of dewdrops and golden thread for girdle.
> (56)

Thus, Ann Cooper Albright, writing a chapter on dance and disability, sets the
dancing body within the context of a European, culturally prestigious milieu,
with the female dancer perceived as an evanescent fairy who moves in a
supernatural world exempt from the restrictions of natural laws. She is at once
romanticized, idealized, and dematerialized.

In contrast, Joann Kealiinnohomoku, writing a chapter on dance and anthropology, cites critical responses to early black dance forms; her examples
clearly show that for the early dance modernists the black dancing body existed
within a racialized African or culturally inferior milieu. Here the black dancer is
not an evanescent fairy that is dematerialized; rather, the black dancer is all too
material, "limited" and "unconscious"; and movement, encoded in "racial
memory," is characterized by a brutality and an "instinctive exuberance" that
are nothing more than the embodiment of natural laws (Copeland 540).

Descriptions such as these demonstrate to what extent dance criticism and
history seem to be entangled in gender and racial assumptions. At once aes-
theticizing and judging dance performance under the cover of critical authority,
such descriptions reflect, reproduce, and maintain the gaps between white and
black dance cultures. The two racialized bodies have historically been placed at
extreme ends of an admittedly unstable and untenable dance aesthetic: one presented as light, ethereal, and refined and the other as dark, brutal, and exotic. In
short, refined "whiteness" became "art," and an excluded "blackness" was
"folk" or ethnic popular culture. A further distinction, one skewed by gender,
resulted in a generally accepted vision of a dancer as "white, female, thin, long-
limbed, flexible, able-bodied" (Albright 57), a distinction that, in fact, dominated the history of dance and predated the dance modernists by more than a
century. By the early twentieth century, this double distinction imprisoned the

black dancing body within the stereotypes that gave a black dancer a false start, if any, in a white dance world.

The widespread belief, present in America since the birth of the nation, in the "naturalness" of the hierarchical differences between the white and the black races has been the basis for various forms of racial discrimination in all realms of public life. It was also a determining factor in the evolution of black dance as a distinct art form. The stereotypical presentation of the black body in dance was to a certain degree triggered by the fact that, as Thomas DeFrantz states, "The black man's body entered American consciousness as a powerful exotic commodity: a slave" (Morris 47). Seen by white masters, first and foremost, as work potential, the black body became immediately associated with exotic movements such as shuffling of the feet, rapid shaking of the shoulders, and much pelvic swaying, and the movements were often described as hideous or lascivious – black dancing bodies were judged by a separate set of aesthetic criteria. The persistence of this nativist perception of black rhythm and excessive energy was furthermore consolidated by the so-called "scientific" definition of race, according to which, as Henry Louis Gates, Jr., puts it, "'race' was a 'thing,' an ineffaceable quantity, which irresistibly determined the shape and contour of human anatomy" (qtd. in Morris 47).

The work of dance critics such as John Martin, with their pseudo-anthropological theories, strengthened the perception of the black body as exotic, putting it constantly in clear opposition to the white body. Using this peculiar vocabulary when describing black artists, those critics determined the public's perception of African American dance. Not only was the tone of the statements patronizing, but the expressions they used were often explicitly and overtly racially biased. Martin, for example, claimed that with their "uniquely racial rhythm," vigor, and particular "proportions of the limbs and torso and the conformation of the feet" (179), black bodies were not adaptable culturally or anatomically to the European dance tradition. "Proved" scientifically inferior to the white standards and seen as predominantly masculine, strong, and physically dynamic, the black dancing body was placed more in the context of physical culture than in the context of art.

One of the strongest sources of racial thinking that undoubtedly added to the way the aesthetics of the black dancing body were perceived and presented was minstrelsy. A caricature of blacks introduced by white artists at the beginning of the nineteenth century, minstrelsy was carried as a stereotype into the twentieth century, appropriating black cultural material for the purpose of ridicule and subjugation. In his recent, much enlightening study of minstrelsy, Eric Lott observes that "there was no attempt at realism" (27) in minstrelsy. On the contrary, white fascination with and fear of black bodies created imaginative projections which paradoxically aimed at both the "othering" of and identification with the dancing body on stage. Based on exaggerated movements of the whole body, such as the swaying of the hips and pelvis, the rolling of the eyes, or the waving of the hands, minstrelsy undoubtedly worked as a negative stereotype in the discourse of racism. However, used as a site of liberation, paradoxically, minstrelsy also provided a stage for signifying among black dancers and performers, who deliberately employed minstrelsy in order to parody it. Similarly, Josephine Baker, although described as one of the "noble savages," struggled against the presentation of black culture as primitive by simultaneously confirming and refuting the perceived notions of the black dancing body in her performances. In this volume, Michael Borshuk's careful analysis of Josephine Baker's early performances in the 1920s and 1930s, *An Intelligence of the Body: Disruptive Parody through Dance in the Early Performances of Josephine Baker*, discusses the strategies Baker used to undermine the stereotypes of black performers, the "damaging constructions of 'blackness.'" Usually misunderstood, at least in her lifetime, as reinforcing the stereotype of the primitive, Baker was a "slippery signifier" who, like many black minstrels, took the stereotype to absurd levels in order to tear it apart and transcend it. Thus Borshuk rereads Baker's performances within the cultural milieu of the 1920s and 1930s as parody, articulating a social criticism through her dancing.

Even the intelligentsia of the Harlem Renaissance in the 1920s misread Baker and the power of dance to expose racial biases, instead feeling that emphasis on the physicality of the black body only served to reinforce what they were working so hard to erase. Wendy Perron's essay in this volume, *Dance in the Harlem Renaissance: Sowing Seeds*, foregrounds dance as an important yet neglected contribution to the Harlem Renaissance, noting that although it thrived in the ballrooms and clubs of Harlem and was an integral part of its cultural life, few scholars then and now have noted its significance. A major reason for this lack of recognition, Perron argues, was that intellectuals of the period like Alain Locke and W.E.B. Du Bois believed that the physicality of dance, "connected as it was to minstrelsy and sexuality," undermined black achievements in literature and the arts, reinforcing the stereotype of blacks as primitive and merely sensual. However, figures like Zora Neale Hurston and Josephine Baker, influenced as they were by the Negro church, valorized dance, pointing to its spiritual and liberating qualities, as did writers like Langston Hughes, Jessie Fauset, and Claude McKay, who, in their poetry and fiction, saw the possibilities for dance to uplift the race.

Likewise, Anthea Kraut, in uncovering Zora Neale Hurston's contribution to American dance, in *Re-scripting Origins: Zora Neale Hurston's Staging of Black Vernacular Dance*, suggests that Hurston's staging of dance has largely remained obscure, citing among the reasons Hurston's uneasy position among the Harlem Renaissance intellectuals and the fact that her literary work has had such an uneven reception over the years. Kraut focuses her attention on the 1932 revue *The Great Day*, where Hurston drew on her anthropological research in the South and the Bahamas in her attempt to alter the audience's under-standing of black vernacular dance. Kraut concludes that Hurston's staging of this folk revue should be considered an inaugural event in the formation of a black concert dance movement.

It was through the anthropological research of choreographers and dancers like Asadata Dafora, Pearl Primus, and Katherine Dunham in the 1930s and 1940s that important steps were taken toward the legitimacy of black aesthetics among both black and white audiences. These artists successfully established their own dance groups, where they applied their field study work to their dances, with the intent of presenting the black tradition in a serious manner. In spite of their efforts, however, critics immediately placed them within the limi-tation of new stereotypes. As a consequence, the works that presented black heritage from the perspective of its African and Caribbean roots unintentionally distanced black dancing from mainstream modern dance. Dance based on an-thropological research in Jamaica, Trinidad, and Haiti that made use of black folk rituals, African chants, costumes, and drum beats was soon labeled by the critics as exotic. Although it did elevate black concert dance to the status of autonomous art, nevertheless, at the same time, they presented black dancers as primitive and exotic creatures, only this time they danced on the legitimate theater stage.

Ramsay Burt's essay in this volume, *Katherine Dunham's "Rites de Passage": Censorship and Sexuality*, proposes that the censoring of the ballet in 1944 in Bos-ton and Dunham's response to the censoring offer insights into an ongoing struggle between Dunham's radical black modernist liberalism and a dominant white social and cultural conservatism. Placing *Rites de Passage* in the context of Dunham's work as a performer, choreographer, and anthropologist, and locating the incident within its social and historical context, Burt reveals the tensions between the expressive power of dance to make positive represen-tations of gender, race, and sexuality and the constraints placed on black cultural expressions by a dominant white society.

In writing about the 1954 Dino De Laurentiis-Carlo Ponti production *Mambo*, Dorothea Fischer-Hornung, in her essay *The Body Possessed: Katherine Dunham's Dance Technique in "Mambo,"* explores how Katherine Dunham's work in a European commercial film signals and enacts the complexity of socially-gendered and racialized identities, arguing that although it seems likely that Dunham's strategy in the film was to enforce the notion that dancing was not something that came naturally to black dancers but an art form that required learned skills and technique, nonetheless the film itself most likely failed to convey this to the viewer. *Mambo* is thus caught between the essentialist per-ception of the audience and Dunham's liberating project.

Even with late post-World-War-II dance experiences of such choreo-graphers as Alvin Ailey, Tally Beatty, or Donald McKayle, the black body still did not have as full degree of aesthetic legitimacy as white performing bodies, that is, those associated with "art." The black body was still seen as odd or exotic. Alvin Ailey, whose list of accomplishments is not equaled by any other black choreographer and whose input in the development of African American aesthetics is inestimable, recalls the situation in these words:

> There were few places for a black man to be a dancer in the early 1940s.... In the 1940s and 1950s the American dance world practiced a pervasive racism. For a variety of reasons: Our feet weren't shaped right, our butts were too big, our legs wouldn't turn out correctly, blacks simply weren't wanted; and so on. The people who ran major and minor ballet companies coldy rejected, and broke the hearts of, many aspiring young dancers. In the dance world, at that time, we were not welcome. (Ailey 51)

Thus, in the early 1960s it was still acceptable for John Martin to write in his *Book of Dance*:

> To cast a Negro as one of a community of Jews in Shalom Aleichem village in Russia, or as a pioneer woman in eighteenth century Appalachia, or as a member of a medieval German prince's hunting party in *Swan Lake*, is to make him conspicuously non-integrated. It is like casting a woman as King Lear or a man as Juliet, and expecting nobody to notice it on the grounds of some spurious sort of politeness. With this art has nothing to do. (189)

Such attitudes were precisely what Ailey was working against. *In (Re)Crossing Borders: The Legacy of Alvin Ailey*, the sixth essay in this collection, Alison D. Goeller analyzes Ailey's remarkable ability to cross and recross aesthetic, gendered, and racial borders as he built the most successful African American dance theater in the history of the United States. Her close reading of Ailey's most well-known piece, *Revelations*, delineates Ailey's ability to politicize the black body and liberate it from the constraints of both the critics' and the public's attitude, while at the same time achieving unprecedented commercial success.

More recently, black dancers have challenged the stereotypical representations of race inherited from the past, disturbing the nineteenth and early twentieth century notions of identity and aesthetics that were created on the basis of racial attributes of the body. Choreographers such as Garth Fagan, Bill T. Jones, Ralph Lemon, and Blondell Cummings address issues that are culturally diverse, such as age, gender, and sexual orientation, and see the world as cross-references of cultures. In the final essay in this collection, *Phoenix Perspectives: African American Influences on a British Dance Company*, Christy Adair traces African American influences, such as the tap dancing Nicholas Brothers, on the Phoenix Dance Company, a contemporary British dance troupe, and explains how notions of agency, including resistance to codes and structures of gender and culture, have also influenced them. Adair recognizes the dilemma of attempting to examine categories related to postmodernity and cultural difference without fixing meaning and the danger of misunderstanding cultural references or of perceiving issues from a viewpoint which is narrowed by an imperialist gaze.

Finally, this collection includes an interview with Isaac Julien, whose pioneering films *Looking for Langston* (1989) and *Young Blood Rebels* (1991) established him as one of the major independent British filmmakers. In this interview conducted with Julien in April 1999, Ramsay Burt and Christy Adair discuss with him one of his latest projects, the dance film and installation *Three*.

We hope that in offering these essays on the black body in American dance we have illustrated how, throughout the history of dance in America, black dancers and choreographers have had to struggle for acceptance in a dominant white aesthetic in order to gain status and legitimacy within the body politic. Measured against such a struggle, their achievements have demonstrated the will and determination of African Americans, who were initially enslaved as "bodies," to liberate themselves via that very body. Thus, the history of black dance in America resembles much of the history of the African diaspora in the Americas: the struggle for acceptance in the dance world, while at the same time, refuting imposed stereotypical representations and obtaining proper aesthetic legitimization. It is fair to say in this context that with its struggle over centuries against physical enslavement, stereotypes, and prejudices, the black body has finally come to represent in dance not only African American experience but also American experience – in this way embodying liberation.

Works Cited

Albright, Ann Cooper. *Choreographing Difference: The Body and Identity in American Dance*. Hanover: Wesleyan UP, 1997.

Copeland, Roger, and Marshall Cohen. *What Is Dance? Readings in Theory and Criticism*. New York: Oxford UP, 1983.

Lott, Eric. "Love and Theft: The Racial Unconscious of Blackface Minstrelsy." *Representations* (Summer 1992): 23–50.

Martin, John. *John Martin's Book of the Dance*. New York: Tudor, 1970.

Morris, Gay, ed. *Moving Words, Re-writing Dance*. New York: Routledge, 1996.

Dance in the Harlem Renaissance:
Sowing Seeds

Wendy Perron

Although in the 1920s and 1930s dance in Harlem was central to its cultural life, rarely has it been recognized as a major contribution to the burgeoning excitement and growing intellectual consciousness that was the Harlem Renaissance. And yet we know from historical accounts that dance was essential to the lives and imaginations of the period. Dance shines through the poetry of Langston Hughes and Claude McKay; it figures importantly in the novels of Jessie Fauset and Nella Larsen; it is a major theme in the paintings of Aaron Douglas. Further, dance of the Harlem Renaissance influenced the development of both black and white dance artists throughout the twentieth century.

As David Levering Lewis, one of the few scholars to acknowledge the presence of dance in the movement, has pointed out, people of all classes went to the big ballrooms – the Savoy, the Renaissance, and the Alhambra. The social dances such as the Shag, the Shimmy, the Grizzly Bear, the Big Apple, the Black Bottom, the Charleston, and the Lindy evolved in Harlem. In night clubs such as Small's Paradise, the Cotton Club, Connie's Inn, and the Plantation, dance was also a big draw, though most often it took the form of black dancers performing for white audiences.

Another important showcase for dance in Harlem was the musical. Because African Americans were effectively banned from Broadway in the 1910s (Emery 213), they developed their own musicals, performing for black as well as white audiences. In 1921 *Shuffle Along* was created by two black men – lyricist Noble Sissle and composer Eubie Blake. James Weldon Johnson, writing in *Black Manhattan*, declared the dancing the "most exhilarating" in the city and called it a "record-breaking, epoch-making musical comedy" (186). This is the show that introduced an unruly chorus girl, Josephine Baker, who later became a sensation in Paris and made Langston Hughes dream of coming to Harlem (Hughes 1940: 62).

Both blacks and whites flocked to *Shuffle Along*, creating such a traffic jam that 63rd Street, where the theater was located, had to be officially declared a one-way street. The dancing included buck and wing (an early version of tap), soft shoe, slow-motion acrobatics, as well as prancing and kicking. A white reviewer described the dancing as follows:

> Every sinew in their bodies danced; every tendon in their frames responded to their extreme energy. They reveled in their work; they simply pulsed with it, and

there was no let-up at all. And gradually, any tired feeling that you might have been nursing vanished in the sun of their good humor. (qtd. in Rose 55)

This elated response explains, in part, the white craze for black music and dance. In addition to the cultural curiosity, it had a concrete effect: it could change one's mood – that is, the mood of white patrons whose lives had become, with the onset of the machine age, increasingly sterile. In *Harlem Renaissance*, Nathan Huggins' re-evaluation of the period, Huggins discusses how black stereotypes fit into white psychic needs:

> Harlem was a means of soft rebellion for those who rejected the ... sterility of their lives, yet could not find within their familiar culture the genius to redefine themselves in more human and vital terms. The Negro was their subversive agent – his music, manners, and speech.... The fantasy of Negro sexuality is fed by deep springs in the white psyche.... Negroes were that essential self one somehow lost on the way to civility, ghosts of one's primal nature whose very nearness could spark electric race-memory of pure sensation untouched by self-consciousness and doubt. (55)

Whites were hungry to recapture the essential, uninhibited self, which they readily projected onto the exhilarating dancing in *Shuffle Along*.

Shuffle Along not only helped create excitement for both whites and blacks, but also had a lasting effect. Huggins credits it with ushering in the Jazz Age (289). Lynne Fauley Emery, in her book *Black Dance: From 1619 to Today*, credits it with popularizing tap dance (223). Jacqui Malone in *Steppin' on the Blues* calls it the most important musical comedy of the twenties (76).

Following *Shuffle Along* was a rash of black musicals, including *Dixie to Broadway*, *Lula Belle*, *Rang Tang*, and *Bamboola*. Even in a show like *Hot Chocolates*, which featured musical greats Fats Waller and Louis Armstrong, dancing was an integral feature (Malone 78).

Dance and the New Negro

Despite the success of these musicals, Harlem intellectuals who promoted the New Negro movement disapproved of black musicals. They felt the characters portrayed were governed by "music, sex, primeval instincts, and an incapacity for logic" (Lewis 92). But European artists were falling in love with things African, and it was, according to Jean-Claude Baker in *Josephine: The Hungry Heart*, the painter Fernand Léger who suggested to impresario Rolf de Maré that he hire African Americans from Harlem for a show (91). Likewise, the German theater director Max Reinhardt had seen *Shuffle Along* and had admired its expressiveness, spontaneity, and rhythm. He felt that these were uniquely

American qualities that could be used to brighten the European scene (Rose 84). Lewis writes that when Charles Johnson and Alain Locke were planning the special edition of the journal *Survey Graphic* that eventually evolved into *The New Negro,* they shared a vision that did not welcome Reinhardt's enthusiasm.

> Both wanted the same art for the same purposes – highly polished stuff, prefera- bly about polished people, but certainly untainted by racial stereotypes or embar- rassing vulgarity. Too much blackness, too much streetgeist and folklore – nitty- gritty music, prose, and verse – were not welcome.... When Max Reinhardt rhapsodized about musicals like *Liza, Shuffle Along,* and *Runnin' Wild,* Johnson and Locke visibly cooled. (Lewis 95)

Johnson and Locke considered the physicality – and sexuality – of the dancing in these shows to be uncultured and therefore had no place in *The New Negro.* As they saw it, dance was not heroic like the sorrow songs so poignantly described by W.E.B. Du Bois in the final chapter of *The Souls of Black Folk.* Locke, in discussing these songs in his chapter on Negro spirituals in *The New Negro,* bemoans the reluctance to elevate these songs – or any folk art – to the level of high art:

> In its ... simplicity, folk art is always despised and rejected at first; but generations after, it flowers again and transcends the level of its origin. The slave songs are no exception; only recently have they come to be recognized as artistically pre- cious things. It still requires vision and courage to proclaim their ultimate value and possibilities. (199)

While Locke and other scholars recognized the significance of the sorrow songs, they did not have the "vision and courage" to recognize dance as art. And yet Locke traces the origin of these beloved spirituals to the "shout" and to dancing in churches.

In *The New Negro* Alain Locke pays lip service to but never specifically discusses dance. He introduces his essay "The Legacy of the Ancestral Arts" in this way:

> Music and poetry, and to an extent the dance, have been the predominant arts of the American Negro. This is an emphasis quite different from that of the African cultures, where the plastic and craft arts predominate. (254)

This quotation demonstrates Locke's misconception about the role of dance in African culture. Perhaps if he had known that dance and music were essential in everyday life in Africa, he would have taken dance more seriously. But Locke, along with most Harlem intellectuals, never set foot in Africa. Crafts and sculptures had been imported from Africa at that time, but not the dances or the music. He had no basis for claiming that one art predominated over the others. Many of us today would view these dances as folk art, deserving of all the attention Locke and Du Bois gave the spirituals. Like the sorrow songs, they attest to the ability of the spirit to soar in the face of oppression. But Locke did not see it that way and thus excluded dance from *The New Negro,* which set the tone and outlined the scope of the Harlem Renaissance. [1]

Whereas dance was cause for embarrassment to Du Bois, Johnson, and Locke, some of the younger writers embraced it. Claude McKay, whose raunchy depiction of blacks in *Home to Harlem* antagonized Du Bois and Locke, loved *Shuffle Along* and felt it was important. He takes issue with the Negro "radicals" headed by Du Bois:

> The Negro radicals of those days were always hard on Negro comedy. They were against the trifling, ridiculous and common side of Negro life presented in artistic form. Radical Negroes take this attitude because Negroes have traditionally been represented on the stage as a clowning race. But I felt that if Negroes can lift clowning to artistry, they can thumb their noses at superior people who rate them as a clowning race. (qtd. in Emery 224)

McKay argues here that clowning – or dancing – when lifted to the level of artistry, can edify the race. That is indeed what Bert Williams, Bill Robinson, Ethel Waters, and Josephine Baker did, in the same way that any artist does: through observation, practice, imagination, craft, dedication, and guts. But the dances expressed buoyancy and sensuality, which were too close to minstrelsy for comfort.

However, another kind of dance, one that was more aligned with the image of the New Negro, was brewing. A young actor, Hemsley Winfield, gathered together a group of largely untrained dancers and formed the Bronze Ballet Plastique, an all-black troupe that performed in Yonkers, New York. In *The Black Tradition in American Dance,* scholar Richard Long reports that Winfield had studied dance with Mikhail Mordkin, the Russian ballet dancer who later established American Ballet Theatre. After reading Locke's *The New Negro,* he changed the name of his group to The New Negro Art Theater Dance Group (see Illus. 4). In 1931 the company performed at Theater in the Clouds, a tiny midtown theater, to packed houses. One dance was based on African themes; another was based on Negro spirituals. Edna Guy danced two solos taught to her by Ruth St. Denis: "Figure from Angkor-Vat" and "Temple Offering" (Long 1989: 25). In 1932 Winfield and Guy performed in a revue partly written by Zora Neale Hurston called "Fast and Furious," forging a connection that might have gone farther had Winfield not died of pneumonia a year later. Three months before his death at twenty-seven, Winfield and his group became the first black dancers to perform at the Metropolitan Opera Company, in *Emperor*

---

[1] Two years later he called vaudeville's dancers and singers the "real mine" of black talent (qtd. in Long 1998: 88).

Jones. Edna Guy later went on to do "dance spirituals" accompanied by Negro spirituals.[2]

The Tradition of the African American Church

The experience of dance is both spiritual and sensual. Many Christian churches, regarding sensuality as dangerous, have banned dance from time to time. But in the black churches, the African tradition of finding one's soul through music and movement superseded the ban (Emery 220). Zora Neale Hurston, one of the literary lights of the Renaissance and a trained anthropologist, studied the traditions of the black church and published her results as *The Sanctified Church*. In it she claims that the southern form of "shouting" continues the tradition of African trance dances in which one is "possessed" by the gods (91). She points out that "all Negro-made church music is dance-possible" (103). In talking about church activities, she explains that "since music without motion is unnatural among Negroes there is always something that approaches dancing – in fact IS dancing – in such a ceremony" (104). She describes services in which people are "saved" in a variety of ways, most of them very physical. These include the violent throwing of arms, jumping up and down, shoulder-shaking, running down the aisle, making faces, and being lifted and carried (92–94).

Interestingly, Josephine Baker, who became known for projecting a brazen sexuality, came out of this church tradition. Phyllis Rose, author of *Jazz Cleopatra: Josephine Baker in Her Time*, recounts the influence of Baker's experiences at "Holy Roller" (Pentecostal) services:

> In this hypnotic setting, one person after another would jump up to demonstrate possession. They entered a kind of stylized trance whose excitement was contagious. The whole congregation stood, eyes closed, swaying, caught up in the ecstatic experience.
>
> Little Josephine ... observed that stylized jumping, running, jerking, and screaming could be signs of something powerful going on inside, and highly acceptable to the group. In the white European tradition, the soul is a quiet thing, to be discovered in peace and through introspection. In the African tradition, the soul can express itself in motion and be discovered through motion. Childhood churchgoing gave Baker the conviction that ... the soul could express itself through the body. (Rose 26-27)

---

[2] Much of the information in this last paragraph comes from conversations I had with Joe Nash between 1999 and 2000.

This passage suggests that Baker's church experience of spirit possession influenced her later movement vocabulary. In contrast to white quietness and stillness of soul, black churchgoers find soul in body motion. This goes back to the African notion of the body as prayer. As dance historian Joe Nash has stated, "One does not simply sing or read a prayer, but one imbues the entire body with spirituality."

Dance as Animal/Sexuality/Temptation

The earthly side of the spiritual in dance is the sensual. For many whites, this aspect is more visible than the spiritual, especially when observing black dance. The idea of black dancing as overly sensual, or "primitive," concurs with the notion of blacks being unfit for civilization, the very notion that made slavery possible. The primitivist aesthetic holds that blacks belong "in the jungle," a view that lends itself to the perception of the sensuality and sexuality of black dance as animality. In the case of Josephine Baker, the perception of her as an animal is best captured in dance critic André Levinson's review of 1927:

> The Negro frenzy, although it is completely devoid of any nobility and almost "pre-human," if not actually bestial, can attain to a positive grandeur. Josephine Baker ... is an extraordinary creature of simian suppleness – a sinuous idol that enslaves and incites mankind. Thanks to her carnal magnificence and her impulsive vehemence, her unashamed exhibition comes close to pathos.... There seemed to emanate from her violently shuddering body, her bold dislocations, her springing movements, a gushing stream of rhythm.... There was a wild splendor and magnificent animality. Certain of Miss Baker's poses, back arched, haunches protruding, arms entwined and uplifted in a phallic symbol, had the compelling potency of the finest examples of Negro sculpture. (74)

Levinson's "discovery" of the magnificence of Baker as an animal in the jungle reflects a colonialist perspective. Levinson is interested in the riches of Baker's body/land, but repulsed by the culture that produced it. He feels that the best use of this beastly talent is to display it for white society, thus lifting it to the level of art.

Levinson was not the only writer who compared Baker to an animal. During the years when she took civilized Paris by storm, she was compared to a panther, snake, giraffe, kangaroo, and hummingbird (Rose 24). She knew that her success depended on the perception of her as close to nature, as purely sexual. She had a genuine affection for animals and always traveled with an assortment of pets. But she also deliberately played into the mystique. For instance, she would walk down the streets of Paris with her pet leopard. She also didn't mind playing the temptress. Whether joking or not, she described her dancing, when it reached a certain pitch, as having the devil in the body – "le diable au corps" (Rose 27). She didn't view sexuality or minstrelsy as vulgar or humiliating. And, as Sally Banes points out in *Dancing Women: Female Bodies on Stage*, Baker "portrayed women, and black women in particular, as sexual subjects with individual dignity, rather than as sexual objects" (157).

Dance in Literature of the Harlem Renaissance

In poetry and in novels of the period, dance held a prominent place. Since *Shuffle Along* was the original inspiration that brought Langston Hughes to New York, it is no surprise that dance appears in many of his poems, as well as in the poetry and fiction of other Renaissance writers. He uses dance to express vitality or a connection to nature. In "Danse Africaine," a veiled girl dances, while the beating of the tom-tom "stirs your blood." Life stirs the blood; sex stirs the blood. In this poem, dance is as basic and essential as life and sex. In two other poems, dance is a moment of pleasure taken against the uncertainty of life. The first of these is "Song for a Banjo Dance":

> Sun's going down this evening
> Might never rise no mo'.
> Sun's going down this very night
> Might never rise no mo'.
> So dance with swift feet, honey,
>   (The banjo's sobbing low)
> Dance with swift feet, honey.
> Might never dance no mo'. (Hughes 1994: 28)

One must find pleasure because it may be the last day the sun rises, the last day of life. For people who have known slavery, perhaps life is even more precarious and more treasured. One's body and soul are treated with such brutality that one might not be able to dance – or breathe – the next day. A shorter poem, "Dancers," expresses much the same sentiment:

> Stealing from the night
> A few
> Desperate hours
> Of pleasure.
>
> Stealing from death

A few
Desperate days
Of life. (Hughes 1994: 334)

Night equals death, and nightclubs are where you fight death with the life that dancing brings. The night's revelry provides a moment of pleasure – whether dancing or sex – for it could be your last. In "Nude Young Dancer," Hughes links dance to animals, both as a connection to nature and as a temptation of sex. He equates dancing in clubs with the jungle (in a bid to reclaim the jungle from white racists like Levinson), opening with "What jungle tree have you slept under, midnight dancer of the jazzy hour?" He connects the dancers with nature, ending the poem with "What star-white moon has been your lover? / To what mad faun have you offered your lips?" (qtd. in Locke 227). Hughes pushes an intimacy with nature close to a Dionysian sense of revelry. Again, dance can bring one toward a paradise of nature, toward one's own sexuality, away from the repressiveness and racism of society.

In the case of Jessie Fauset's novel *There Is Confusion*, dance is a profession. Joanna, the main character, is an ambitious, controlled and calculating woman, and dance is a deliberate part of her life plan. A proud person, she tolerates the humiliation of having to arrange her dance lessons separately from whites. Moreover, dance as a career is seen as an obstacle to love. Her would-be lover, Peter, flares up when she cites dancing as the reason to avoid marriage (133). But by the end of the novel, when Joanna loses her rigid idealism (though not her elitism), she loses her interest in dance, too. In a disappointingly unliberated solution, she opts to drop dance to devote herself to marriage. Dance is finally only a cog in the wheel of Joanna's ambition. It is fitting that, in Fauset's universe (for she was a disciple and colleague of Du Bois) dance is subservient to social ambition.

In Nella Larsen's *Quicksand*, dance provides two turning points – revelations actually – for protagonist Helga Crane. The first is when, as a guest in Denmark, she joins a white audience at a vaudeville show. In the final act, two black performers "danced and cavorted," and the audience responds with wild enthusiasm (82). Their performance is a grotesque exhibit, and Helga, a sensitive woman of mixed race, sees an unsettling glimmer of familiarity in it. She is horrified by both the show and the audience response. "She felt shamed, betrayed, as if these pale pink and white people among whom she lived had suddenly been invited to look upon something in her which she had hidden away and wanted to forget" (83). However, she is drawn to the show again and again in order to contemplate, on her own, what it means to her. So this is why her Danish hosts dress her up in bright-colored outfits. She is a curiosity, an animal in the zoo, and can be nothing more to them. The cruel irony is that she, Helga, has devoted her life to being tasteful, sexually restrained, educated, sophisticated.

And now she is reduced to being a minstrel. Soon after, she decides to return to Harlem, where she can be herself – or at least one half of herself – without being stared at.

The second revelation occurs when, desperate, weak and nauseous, Helga finds herself in a church. She recoils at the spectacle of people jumping "in wild, ecstatic fury" (Larsen 113). Larsen's description here echoes Hurston's dance-like scenes of the sanctified church. Because of Helga's vulnerable state, and almost against her will, she succumbs to being "saved." The ensuing calm enables her to embark on a more stable life. She marries and settles down, only to enter into another kind of bleakness. Although Helga begins and ends the novel in the unbearable state of not even daring to know her own desires, these two episodes bring her momentarily closer to her true self. But ultimately, they intensify her feelings of alienation.

For Claude McKay, on the other hand, dance brings true abandon. In his poem "Negro Dancers," one dances to lose oneself, to blot out the burdens of the everyday world: "Dancing, their world of shadow to forget." And later, "Dead to the earth and her unkindly ways of toil and strife/ For them the dance is the true joy of life." Like the shadow world, the toiling and striving refer to the African American plight. The "true joy" is a joy that is blind to the "shadow" – a moment of ecstasy that releases one from white society's oppression of darker peoples. The dancing has "Not one false step, no note that rings not true" (qtd. in Locke 214). It is also "true" because one does it freely, not to impress anyone, and it brings one closer to one's true self. (This predates Martha Graham's famous dictum that "Movement never lies.") McKay felt that physicality, more than words, reaches the heart and enables one to forget about skin color and the social burden associated with it. He also wishes he could forget. When he says, "They dance with poetry in their eyes," he seems to feel the same way about dancing that Du Bois and Locke felt about the sorrow songs – that they go directly to the soul and in so doing are elevated to an art.

The truth of dancing, born of necessity, is only possible by blotting out the reality of white racism. The question arises whether dance can sustain its truth while being exhibited to white power, as it was in the ballrooms and clubs of Harlem. Hughes felt that the dancers at the Savoy started doing acrobatic moves for white audiences that they would not have done on their own (Hughes 1997: 226). However, dance historian Joe Nash feels that these developments and embellishments were an inevitable outcome of the creative energy and competitiveness of the dancers.

Dance in the Visual Arts

Aaron Douglas was the most prominent visual artist representing the New Negro. Like Hughes and Hurston, he was, for a time, supported by white patron Charlotte Mason, but he never let her control his decisions. Amy Kirschke writes in her biography, *Aaron Douglas: Art, Race, and the Harlem Renaissance*, "Douglas was obviously impressed by Mason's wealth and pleased that she would purchase his work. But the Godmother's influence did not distort his artistic work or his career" (38). He created the designs for several covers of *Crisis*, the magazine of the NAACP, and was chosen to illustrate *The New Negro* (see Illus. 1). His beliefs in the social role of black people were in tune with the New Negro movement:

> The Negro had a new dual role in society, that of acting as the advance guard of the African peoples in their contact with twentieth-century civilization, while also rehabilitating the race in world esteem from that loss of prestige for which fate and the conditions of slavery had been largely responsible. (Kirschke 19)

Douglas, like Locke and Du Bois, believed that art should lift up the image of the Negro in order to compensate for the humiliation of slavery. But unlike Locke and Du Bois, he felt that dance was a part of that uplift. In a paper called "The Negro in American Culture," he wrote:

> The dance offered a field for the unrestricted expression of the Negroes' creative passion. Here were no expensive instruments to be purchased, no weird symbols to be mastered, no unfamiliar tools and stubborn material to be overcome, only swift feet, strong legs, a lust for life and a soaring imagination. With this limited equipment the Negro has kept folk dancing alive in America when it has died almost everywhere else in the world. He has not only kept the dance alive, but in a spontaneous, revolutionary, creative state. (Baigell 79)

Perhaps Douglas' grandest ode to dance is a large mural called "The Evolution of Negro Dance" created for the Harlem YMCA. Still visible on the wall of what is now the Y's hair-dressing salon, his characteristic images are evident: the silhouetted figures dancing in profile and an environment that is ambiguous enough to suggest either a grassland or a nightclub. Though it is now badly in need of restoration, one can still see the stylized shapes and shrewd composition.

Many of his other paintings depict dancing, not necessarily as the central focus, but as an assist in a kind of story or image. These include "The Prodigal Son," "The Congo," "Dance Magic," and "The Negro in an African Setting." In "The Prodigal Son" dance is shown along with money, music, and women as temptations of modern life (Kirschke 99). "The Congo" portrays several women dancers, possibly nude, seen as though through a haze, responding to some unseen whirlwind. It could be a possession dance, where the spiritual and sensual meet. In "Dance Magic" we see a single woman dancing in a nightclub, wearing provocative tassels. In these works, there is no differentiation between social dancing and stage dancing. A deliberate ambiguity keeps the viewer hovering between a "jungle" environment and a stage or nightclub (an urban jungle?), merging the old world with the new.

Other works portray figures who look like dancers, partly due to Douglas' Egyptian and Cubist influences. The figures are open, angular, with stretched, shaped limbs. In some of them, we see not only dance, but expert staging, as in "Sahdji" and "I Couldn't Hear Nobody Pray," where a solo figure is counterpointed by a group. The figures are so clear in their outlines and the groupings are so well composed, one feels one is seeing skillful choreography frozen in time.

Innovation

Although the poets and visual artists liked to depict dance as close to nature, the actual steps are, of course, made up by men or women. In both social and artistic dancing, innovation was a prevailing ethic of the period. According to Marshall and Jean Stearns in *Jazz Dance: The Story of American Vernacular Dance,* "Nobody was permitted to copy anybody else's steps exactly" (322). At the Savoy Ballroom, famous for its social dancing, "individual expression and inventiveness were as prized as technical virtuosity" (Malone 101). "Eccentric dancers" had to create an individual style in order to survive. A good example is Bill "Bojangles" Robinson, known to us as the tap-dancing elder in the popular Shirley Temple movies of the 1950s. Robinson had become a top name in black vaude-ville through constant experimentation (see Illus. 1). In NBC-TV's "Positively Black" series, band leader Cab Calloway said about Robinson, "Everything he came up with he made himself" (McNeill). Critic Robert Benchley called his quality "indescribably liquid, like a brook flowing over pebbles" (qtd. in Stearns 156). Robinson brought tap dancing onto the toes, changing it from the flat-footed buck dancing, making his famous stair dance a wonder of complexity and of ingenuity (Stearns 151).

There were other eccentric dancers who combined elements to create a unique amalgam of steps. For example, Eddie Rector combined new rhythms with a free-flowing style that covered space (Stearns 163, 166). Johnnie Hudgins used Chaplinesque head and arms with slides of the feet (Stearns 146). He also found a way of "turning himself into a human trumpet," according to commentator Margo Jefferson (35). Earl "Snake Hips" Tucker (see Illus. 1), who performed at Connie's Inn and the Cotton Club, was famous for his undulating hips, full-bodied belly roll, and a tremble that racked his body from head to foot (Stearns 237).

Improvisation was used in both social and stage dancing. The Stearns report that at rent-parties close-dancing couples would do the Slow Drag, and each couple would improvise their own variations (Stearns 323). Later, the Lindy introduced the breakaway, in which partners unfold away from each other, adding their own steps (Stearns 323). In describing rehearsals for shows on the T.O.B.A. circuit (the black vaudeville circuit), Malone points out that the directors and dancers "helped cultivate an atmosphere that encouraged improvisation on a wide scale" (81). As end-girl in *Shuffle Along*, Josephine Baker kept the basic steps, but added "crazy things" (Stearns 134). Like a jazz musician, she built her episodes through improvisation (then called "ad lib"):

> What made her special was not routine but improvisation. She was a jazz artist, and her inspired solos, while they took place in a context that had its own discipline, were great because of her gift for spontaneous invention. (Rose 60)

Black Dancing as Source for White Dancing

As in early minstrel days, the dancing of blacks served as source material for white entertainers. According to Long, in his essay "Dance Dimensions" from his collection *Grown Deep: Essays on the Harlem Renaissance*, the impresario Florenz Ziegfield bought a dance routine from *Darktown Follies* for the Ziegfield Follies in 1914 (Long 85; Stearns 125). White producers in the late twenties realized that "the Negro was an inexhaustible source" (Stearns 163). Many black dancers earned a living teaching white students. White dance stars who took lessons with black teachers included Ray Bolger, Adele Astaire and Irene Castle (Stearns 167, 164, 128). Elvis Presley's pelvic thrusts have been called a pale version of Snake Hips Tucker (Stearns 3)[3]. And the mainstream movie musicals of the fifties feature black dances without blacks; for example, scores of dancers do the Charleston in *Singin' in the Rain*, not one of them black. Buddy Bradley, a dancer, teacher, coach, and choreographer, worked on many musicals for white audiences. He helped Hollywood giant Busby Berkeley on a few films, without credit. He collaborated with Anton Dolin, Frederick Ashton, and Leonide Massine; his students included Lucille Ball, Eleanor Powell, Paul Draper, Fred and Adele Astaire and Mae West (Long 1989: 38).

In her essay "Balanchine and Black Dance," Banes tells us that Balanchine collaborated with Bradley on a revue in London in 1931, before arriving in the

---

[3]   Perhaps the "roll" in Rock n Roll is a descendant of the "roll" in Holy Rollers.

United States. Even earlier, in 1926, Balanchine created a part for himself in "The Triumph of Neptune," in which he donned blackface for a solo that borrowed from the cakewalk. He also worked with Josephine Baker during that period. Banes maintains that "he incorporated his deep and abiding love for African-American dancing into the very heart of his technique and choreography" (Banes 1994: 58-69).

Other major white dance artists paid attention to the dancing in Harlem. Just as George Gershwin listened to Fats Waller and James P. Johnson, choreographers Jack Cole, Frederick Ashton, and Jerome Robbins came up to the Savoy and the Apollo to see the dancing (Watson 109). Cole choreographed many musicals in films and on Broadway; his fusion of jazz and modern dance influenced black concert choreographers Alvin Ailey and Talley Beatty as well as white Broadway directors Bob Fosse and Michael Kidd. Ted Shawn was influenced by black dance forms when he choreographed "Juba" (1921), in which Martha Graham danced, and "Crapshooter" (1925), danced by Charles Weidman (Long 1989: 29). And in 1999, Trisha Brown choreographed a dance based on the documentary films that Mura Dehn shot at the Savoy in the 1930s and 40s.

The Marginalization of Dance

When PBS aired its series "I'll Make Me a World" in 1999, they showed clips of Josephine Baker while the credits flashed, but the narrator did not mention her once during the six-hour documentary. The Facets video catalogue's special Black History Month edition of 1999 flaunts Baker on the cover. But search as one might inside, there are no videos of hers and only seven total on dance – out of approximately 700 videos.

As we have seen, dance had a central role in the Harlem Renaissance, but this role is usually not recognized either during the Renaissance or afterward. Dance was not supported the way other arts were. For example, in 1922, the Harmon Foundation (associated with the Federal Council of Churches) established a Negro awards program to stimulate creative work "in education, fine arts, literature, music, industry, science, religion, and for race relations" (Kirschke 39). Note that dance is missing from this list. In later scholarly studies, for example Cheryl Wall's *Women of the Harlem Renaissance*, dance is not discussed (though Baker is mentioned). Neither Huggins nor Lewis mention dance, other than incidentally, in their scholarly treatments of the Renaissance.

Of the Renaissance scholars, only two give dance an equal place with other arts. The first is James Weldon Johnson, who, very early on, in his 1912 treatment of race issues, *The Autobiography of an Ex-Coloured Man*, exulted in the

beauty of the cakewalk. He deemed this dance one of the great accomplishments of the race, along with sorrow songs and ragtime music:

> It is my opinion that the coloured people of this country have done four things
> which refute the oft-advanced theory that they are an absolutely inferior race,
> which demonstrate that they have originality and artistic conception, and, what is
> more, the power of creating that which can influence and appeal universally. The
> first two of these are the Uncle Remus stories ... and the Jubilee songs... The
> other two are rag-time music and the cake-walk.... These are lower forms of art,
> but they give evidence of a power that will some day be applied to the higher
> forms. (87)

And many decades later, Richard Long makes a case for dance being a major
contributor to our culture:

> Black dance in its exalting and spirit-enhancing role in African life and in its
> utilitarian but also redemptive role in the folk life of the Diaspora is one of the
> great creations of the human spirit. (1998: 93)

Legacy

The legacy of the Harlem Renaissance in the concert dance field can be seen in
three ways. First, as stated by Joe Nash, "Winfield and Guy initiated the whole
movement involving African Americans in modern dance."[4] This movement
includes Asadata Dafora, Katherine Dunham, Pearl Primus, Donald McKayle,
Alvin Ailey, Dianne McIntyre, Bill T. Jones, and Jowale Willa Jo Zollar. In
addition, as I have discussed, black dancers sowed seeds for the development of
white choreographers Cole, Ashton, Robbins, Balanchine and others.

Second, as a cultural awakening, the Renaissance had a broad influence on
many types of artists. Dance scholar John O. Perpener, III, in his essay "African
American Dance and Sociological Positivism During the 1930s," contends that
the values of the literary figures seeped through to the aspiring dancers:

> African American concert dancers were among the artists who were influenced
> by the idea that their work should serve a self-consciously sociological function
> as well as aesthetic ends. Artists such as Hemsley Winfield, Asadata Dafora, and
> Katherine Dunham were motivated by the idea that they were not only individ-
> ual artists but first and foremost representatives of their race. (25)

Thus the ideal of the artist advancing the race, as set by the New Negro movement, inspired black dancers and artists of the next generation. Dunham, like

---

4   Conversations with Joe Nash

Hurston (though from a separate route), became an anthropologist and investigated folk forms to ultimately use them as a source for creating art. The kinds of body movements that Hurston wrote about in *The Sanctified Church* – the rituals and body shudderings of being possessed – are similar to what Dunham utilized in her 1945 masterpiece *Shango* (see Pennebaker video). And Pearl Primus, in 1943, named one of her dances after the Langston Hughes' poem that signaled the dawn of a new consciousness among young black poets, "The Negro Speaks of Rivers" (Long 1989: 76).

Third, as I have mentioned, major white dance artists were heavily influenced by what they learned from black dancers.

Throughout the Harlem Renaissance the ideals of the "planters" of the New Negro movement clashed with the younger artists' wish to portray life in its fullest. The former placed art in the service of the advancement of the Negro race and were anxious to leave minstrelsy, and anything remotely resembling it, behind. The latter wanted to be free to delve into their individual imaginations. The New Negro intellectuals felt that the physicality of dance, connected as it was to minstrelsy and sexuality, undermined black achievements in literature and scholarship. Dance was part of a cluster of activities that embarrassed them, including gambling and drinking. But dance enriched people's lives and art. It was a reminder of their ancestors' will to survive, their spirit in the face of hard times. It was a statement of freedom, of the truth of the body, of the link between spirituality and the flesh. It communicated the vitality of the African American culture as exuberantly as jazz music did and generated changes in the art of dance in general. But dance reminded the striving Renaissance scholars of the old Negro, the pre-literary Negro. But then so did Zora Neale Hurston, who valued the folk dialect and customs of the rural uneducated.

As we look back and witness the perception of Hurston and others being revised, perhaps we should also revise our vision of the place of dance in the Harlem Renaissance. Partly because of the ideas of the twenties, dance artists today have a full array of possibilities, and the results are far more complex than in the twenties. Dance as spiritual or racial uplift, dance as pleasure, dance as celebration, dance as sexuality, dance as struggle, dance as freedom, dance as thought, dance as individuality – these are but a few of the possibilities. We can now admire the daring, originality and complexity of work within the confines available to black dancers of the time, and we can see how dance in the Harlem Renaissance sowed seeds for the dancing that enlivens us today.

Works Cited

Baigell, Matthew, and Julia Williams, eds. *Artists against War and Fascism*. New Brunswick: Rutgers U P, 1986. (originally published as Papers of the American Artists' Congress in 1936).

Baker, Jean-Claude, and Chris Chase. *Josephine: The Hungry Heart*. New York: Random House, 1993.

Banes, Sally. *Dancing Women: Female Bodies on Stage*. London: Routledge, 1998.

—. *Writing Dancing in the Age of Postmodernism*. Hanover: Wesleyan UP, 1994.

Douglas, Ann. *Terrible Honesty: Mongrel Manhattan in the 1920s*. New York: Farrar, Noonday, 1995.

Du Bois, W.E.B. *The Souls of Black Folk*. 1903. New York: Doubleday, 1989.

Emery, Lynne Fauley. *Black Dance: From 1619 to Today*. Princeton: Dance Horizons, 1988.

Fauset, Jessie Redmon. *There Is Confusion*. 1924. Boston: Northeastern UP, 1989.

Frank, Rusty. *Tap! The Greatest Tap Dance Stars and Their Stories 1900–1955*. New York: Da Capo P, 1990.

Huggins, Nathan Irvin. *Harlem Renaissance*. London: Oxford UP, 1973.

Hughes, Langston. *The Big Sea*. 1940. New York: Hill, 1997.

—. *The Collected Poems of Langston Hughes*. New York: Random House, 1994.

Hurston, Zora Neale. *The Sanctified Church*. New York: Marlowe, 1981.

Jefferson, Margo. "Glimpses of a Lost Theatrical World." *The New York Times* 20 Oct. 1996, A & L, 35.

Johnson, James Weldon. *Black Manhattan*. 1927. New York: Da Capo P, 1991.

—. *The Autobiography of an Ex-Coloured Man*. 1912. New York: Hill and Wang, 1995.

Kirschke, Amy Helene. *Aaron Douglas: Art, Race, and the Harlem Renaissance*. Jackson: UP of Mississippi, 1995.

Larsen, Nella. *Quicksand and Passing*. New Brunswick: Rutgers UP, 1988.

Levinson, André. *André Levinson on Dance: Writings from Paris in the Twenties*. Ed. Joan Acocella and Lynn Garafola. Hanover: Wesleyan UP, 1991.

Lewis, David Levering. *When Harlem Was in Vogue*. 1979. New York: Penguin, 1997.

Locke, Alain, ed. *The New Negro*. 1925. New York: Simon and Schuster, 1997.

Long, Richard A. *The Black Tradition in American Dance*. London: Prion, 1989.

—. *Grown Deep: Essays on the Harlem Renaissance*. Florida.: FOUR-G, 1998.

Malone, Jacqui. *Steppin' on the Blues: The Visible Rhythms of African American Dance*. Urbana: U of Illinois P, 1996.

McNeill, Harry, producer. "I Knew the Man Bojangles" from the "Positively Black" series, WNBC-TV, 1990.

Nash, Joe, interview with the author, Feb. 1, 1999.

—. interview with the author, Feb. 19, 1999.

Pennebaker, D.A., and Chris Hegedus, producers. *Dance Black America.* TV special based on a performance series held at Brooklyn Academy of Music in 1983, produced in 1984.

Perpener, John O., III. "African American Dance and Sociological Positivism During the 1930s." *Journal of the Society of Dance History Scholars,* 5.1 (1994). 23–30.

Rose, Phyllis. *Jazz Cleopatra: Josephine Baker in Her Time.* New York: Random House, 1991.

Stearns, Marshall, and Jean. *Jazz Dance: The Story of American Vernacular Dance.* 1968. New York: Da Capo P, 1994.

Wall, Cheryl A. *Women of the Harlem Renaissance.* Bloomington: Indiana UP, 1995.

Watson, Steven. *The Harlem Renaissance: Hub of African American Culture, 1920–1930.* New York: Pantheon, 1995.

An Intelligence of the Body: Disruptive Parody through Dance in the Early Performances of Josephine Baker

Michael Borshuk

The *ersatz* jungle. A skirt of bananas. The nearly-nude woman with the *café au lait* skin. A comic figure with dancing eyes, a vibrant smile. A limber agent of liquid movement, in constant motion, in constant transformation – shifting across the stage to the lively rhythms of early jazz. Performance as resistance; dance as the embodiment of disruptive play. Josephine Baker.[1]

With this paper, I read parodic intentions behind Josephine Baker's controversial early performances of the 1920s and 30s. I argue that the chameleon manner and the dance movements she exhibited onstage were strategic. Baker used a calculated slipperiness amidst a variety of cultural contexts to undermine damaging constructions of "blackness." In the sections that follow, I explore the nature of contemporary representations and stereotypes with which Baker played and suggest traditions in African American culture, approaches in contemporary African American criticism, and concepts from related gender studies concerning performance, through which I (re)read various (mis)readings of Baker's performances. Baker's early career marks an intriguing intersection of ostensible compromise and stealthy self-empowerment. Her work capitalized on the notion that, as Richard Dyer has written, "it is not stereotypes, as an aspect of human thought and representation, that are wrong, but who controls and defines them, what interests they serve" (12). Moreover, her performances played with the fact that, as Homi Bhabha has argued, stereotypes are inherently ambivalent, discursive representations of an "'otherness' which is at once an object of desire and derision" for collective bodies of colonizing power (67). Baker constructed herself within a network of injurious representations and exploited her position within this matrix to subversive effect. She was able to diminish the negative power of governing stereotypes and discursive impositions by situating herself at the exaggerated limits of those distorted representations, thus revealing the illegitimacy of white-concocted notions of Negro primitivism and eroticism by situating them within the self-consciously illusory spectacle of the stage.

Often observers posit that Baker was constructed to be, at varying times, a symbol of sensualism, primitivism, and unbound sexuality. Moreover, critics

[1] I would like to express my gratitude to Teresa Zackodnik, Russell Chace, and Heather Zwicker, all of whom read drafts of this essay (or conversed with me about the ideas contained therein) and offered valuable criticisms and suggestions.

have lambasted Baker for her ostensible pliancy and the supposed ease with which she allowed these various constructions to advance. For instance, Fatimah Tobing Rony writes that Baker has been criticized "as an agent of minstrelsy and a toady to whites" (Rony 199) for her appearances as a naked exotic, a beautiful beast in the sexualized jungle fantasies of the French music-hall stage.[2] Such censure constructs her as a wholly malleable figure: an object of desire and influence who could be made to play the Other in the collective fantasy of the white imagination. This gross misconception is representative of what Patricia Williams identifies as the concept of a "black antiwill": the discursive legacy of slavery's rhetoric of white paternalism, a continuing belief in the absence of self-reliance among African Americans (219–20). While commentators who posit that Baker was the object of control exhibit a faith in this antiwill through their negation of any intention on Baker's part, her slipperiness complicates such a reading.

Baker appeared to have cultivated a version of the premeditated ambiguity that Ann Douglas argues was a popular strategy of resistance among black performers in the 1920s:

> The chosen mode of black Manhattan was one of contrasting, shifting rhythms as a fractured but infinite series of improvisations never culminating in the denouement of unmasking.... Disguise was so necessary to the black performer that final unmasking, stasis, "telling it straight," ... became the ultimate taboo.... Harlem's greatest natural resource, its birthright art of expressiveness, also constituted its most self-conscious and strategic defense. The black moderns were perhaps the supreme players in the masquerade that was 1920s Manhattan culture, players whose disguises were doubly necessary ones that could not be, and were not intended to be, fully decoded by their white audiences and collaborators.... (105–06)

Too often, Baker's critics overlook her savvy for constructing her own image and ignore the creative agency of her performances, arguing that her early career marks a recurring act of apostatization – a selling-out of her "blackness" for superficial personal gain. They rarely see her chameleon quality as a result of her own careful fluidity or a desire to remain forever slippery and unfixed.

Defined by this fluidity, Baker's performances teased the colonial fantasy. They appeared to coalesce with the conceptions of the exotic that reigned in the

---

2   For example, in *Jazz Cleopatra* Phyllis Rose quotes Will Marion Cook's 1925 review of the *Revue Nègre* in which he lambastes the show as a distorted representation of real black culture and opines: "The prostituting of Negro talent by encouraging imitation of all that is weak, low, and vicious must stop.... From now on let's have the real thing" (qtd. in Rose 80). Cook was a composer whom Alain Locke later credited as giving "Negro music its first serious orchestral ambitions" (qtd. in Floyd 7). His sentiments here implicitly echo the dismissal of the African American popular arts by the Harlem Renaissance intelligentsia which I discuss later.

white imagination, yet ultimately proved to be caricatures of those very idealizations. Though Baker played both Vietnamese and African colonials in love with French colonists in sketches from the *Folies Bergère* between 1930 and 1933, in the end Baker was as much a "Western" figure as those spectators in her audience: a master of the modern dances, a flapper with treated hair. And while she may have acted like a beast or a primitive onstage – appearing, for example, as an overgrown dragonfly pursued by white hunters in another of the *Folies* 1930–31 tableaux – Baker was just as likely to appear in formal wear among the cultural elite at Zelli's when the evening's final curtain had fallen. Baker's juxtaposition effectively deconstructed what Anne McClintock defines as one of the guiding rationalizations of colonialism: namely, the belief that the colonized Other's present is an "anachronistic space," parallel to an earlier, less civilized stage in Western history that contradicts the enlightened present in which Europeans exist (40). As McClintock writes, "Imperial progress across the space of empire is figured as a journey backward in time to an anachronistic moment of prehistory"(40).[3] Baker collapsed the trope by juxtaposing "modernity" and "prehistory" in herself, revealing those ostensibly divided notions to exist in the same geographical place, on the same temporal plane. She never attempted a mere reversal of damaging conventions; rather, her shows seemed to confirm stereotypes so they could tear them apart. She herself later said, "Since I personified the savage on the stage, I tried to be as civilized as possible in daily life" (qtd. in Baker and Bouillon 55). In perpetuating this juxtaposition – between what her public wanted her to be and how she appeared instead – she became the "always almost" object of the colonial fantasy, a calculated fraud that exposed the whole order as a sham.

Historically, though, commentators have undervalued the ingenuity of Baker's performances and overlooked the subversive intentions I read here.[4] Her medium is the curse, perhaps, in this regard; her critics have possibly underrated the potential for politics amidst the swinging music and frantic dancing of the French music hall, which thrived on an ostensible reaffirmation of negative representations. A critical (re)reading of her performances, which theorizes

---

[3] As McClintock explains in *Imperial Leather*, the idea of anachronistic space was used in the late Victorian era to disavow "the agency of women, the colonized and the industrial working class" and project them as "prehistoric, atavistic and irrational, inherently out of place in the historical time of modernity" (40). Baker thus seems all the more disruptive here in her simultaneous embodiment of the three positions that this idea seeks to regulate: woman, oppressed racial Other, working class subject.

[4] For recent exceptions to this kind of reading see Wendy Martin's "'Remembering the Jungle': Josephine Baker and Modernist Parody"; Nancy Nenno's "Femininity, the Primitive, and Modern Urban Space: Josephine Baker in Berlin"; and Karen C. C. Dalton and Henry Louis Gates, Jr.'s "Josephine Baker and Paul Colin: African American Dance Seen through Parisian Eyes."

parodic agency in her work, necessitates a review of the cultural milieu in which she performed and the received notions she challenged.

During the 1920s and 30s, for example, African American intellectuals repeatedly undervalued the importance of black popular entertainment in their hierarchization of the African American arts. The so-called "low" arts were suspiciously excluded from the unofficial race-advancement project that was being promoted by the black intelligentsia during the Harlem Renaissance. The Renaissance's triumvirate of self-styled leadership – W.E.B. Du Bois, Alain Locke and James Weldon Johnson – distinguished between literary writers, classical musicians and actors in the "legitimate" theatre on the one side and jazz and pop musicians as well as entertainers in musical theatre on the other (Floyd 18). The tacit theory behind the demarcation was that blacks could improve their status only by showing a refined face to whites, by forging a collective cultural product that was on par with the best of the European and Euro-American traditions.[5] Yet in the end, this concession to white European aesthetics led to a depreciation of the African American folk and popular arts; it misread them as the trivial commodities of white consumption. Primitivism was especially key to this misreading. As Baker's career in show business began, the *Zeitgeist*'s fascination with the Negro's inherently "primitive" demeanor bore meaningful influence on American arts and popular entertainment. Through their particular experience black Americans had forged a distinct lifestyle and a variant set of cultural values which whites read as essential difference. Thus, as Nathan Huggins writes, by the 1920s blacks "could serve a new kind of white psychological need" (89). Whites imagined that observation of, and interaction with, African Americans might take them back to an earlier, less complicated stage in their evolution. White sponsorship and spectatorship of the black arts offered a convenient avenue through which this psychological need might be satisfied.[6] In Harlem nightclubs like the Cotton Club and Connie's Inn, for instance, a voyeuristic economy informed by the cult of primitivism was repeatedly constructed between white patrons and the blacks in attendance. For whites, the black popular arts appeared to harness the "primitive" spirit of the Negro and offer an opportunity to acquire a version of the jungle without sacrificing white civility through the negotiation.

Josephine Baker, who had worked for a short time in the Plantation Club, one of the numerous white-trade Harlem clubs in the strip that came to be nicknamed "Jungle Alley," brought this phenomenon to France and utilized it.

---

[5]   As Alain Locke wrote in the introduction to his seminal work, *The New Negro* (1925): the "immediate hope [for improving the conditions of African Americans] rest[ed] in the revaluation by white and black alike of the Negro in terms of his artistic endowments and cultural contributions" (15).

[6]   For more detailed accounts of this relationship between modernism and the primitive in 1920s pop culture, see Huggins, especially pp. 87–88, and Douglas, especially Chapter 7.

Her early performances in Paris repeatedly embodied the jungle motif that was raging in Harlem and in some cases took it to daring new extremes. Baker's initial moment onstage in the *Revue Nègre* in 1925, for example, presented her in the first of many variations on this theme. Dressed in rags, Baker made her entrance as a clowning, vaguely animal figure. Emerging sinuous and cartoonly feral onstage, she was later compared to a variety of beasts in a review of the show in the newspaper *Candide*: "a boxing kangaroo," "a snake," "a young giraffe" (qtd. in Baker and Bouillon 55). And as the program advanced, Baker evoked the primitive spirit still more. The show's finale was a curious exhibition that summed up the presumed intersection between animal vivacity and urbane nightlife back in Harlem and, as such, offered white audiences more commodified savagery tempered by artifice. Against a backdrop designed to resemble one of Jungle Alley's jazzy nightclubs, Baker returned bare-breasted with feathers around her waist and neck, in her hair, and on her ankles. She was carried in atop the shoulders of a dancing partner whom Janet Flanner later remembered as "a black giant": Joe Alex, outfitted in beads and feathers himself (Flanner xx). Together they danced the Danse Sauvage, in which Baker began belly-down on Alex's back, in a kind of lurching handstand, before shimmering to her stomach on the floor, sliding into what Phyllis Rose writes was "probably an improvised combination of various moves related to the Belly Dance – the Shake, the Shimmy, the Mess Around.... Not a Charleston, danced with the legs and the arms, it was a dance for the rear end" (21). The "primitive" nature of the climactic dance was not lost on *Candide*'s reviewer: Baker, with her "arms high, belly thrust forward, buttocks quivering," took the audience "back to primeval times" (qtd. in Baker and Bouillon 55).[7] In all, her variations on the jungle theme extended the contemporary relationship between white specularity and black onstage performance. Ultimately, Baker's body became the quintessential referent for the dramatization of the Negro's primitive spirit. However, though she was pushing the jungle spectacle to an outrageously unprecedented apex, the perverse curiosity on which she played was hardly novel. As Sander L. Gilman has documented, whites had been scrutinizing the black woman's body to observe its difference for over a century. In his work, "Black Bodies, White

---

[7] For years after that, the jungle drama continued. Baker repeatedly embodied the black's purported animal spirit in her onstage dance routines. In her 1926 debut at the *Folies Bergère* she "made her entrance through an electric twilight walking backward on her hands and feet, arms and legs stiff, along the thick limb of a painted jungle tree and down the trunk, like a monkey" (Rose 97). As the scene progressed, she broke into her savage dance from the *Revue Nègre*, this time performed *sans* Joe Alex, with a white dancer dressed as a hunter observing her from onstage. Her costume in that production was the most famous one she ever wore: a skirt of bananas that played with the simian motif all the more. Yet she certainly played more than monkeys: in *Folies* shows that followed, her bestial "self" took avis and feline forms as well.

Bodies: Toward an Iconography of Female Sexuality in Late Nineteenth-Century Art, Medicine, and Literature," Gilman documents how nineteenth century artistic representation and scientific discourse built upon a convention from the previous century that situated "the sexuality of the black, both male and female … [as] an icon for deviant sexuality in general," with the black female body as a more specific symbol for black sexuality (228, 231).

The black female body in the nineteenth century was perceived as emblematic of a purportedly "primitive" sexual disposition (Gilman 232). Fascination over sexual difference between the races fed European interest in scrutinizing the black woman's body. A defining example of the black female's iconographic status is the public fascination with the 1810 London "exhibition" of Saartjie Baartman, also called Sarah Bartmann or Saat-Jee, an indentured black known as the "Hottentot Venus" (Gilman 232). Through her public display, the black woman became the sexualized object of a prurient speculation – stripped of agency and reduced to her parts – that would continue after the *fin de siècle*. The early twentieth century remained perpetually absorbed with the black female body. The black woman's sexuality was constructed as an emblem of deviance; her libido was perceived as a naturally uncontained drive that might prove perilous if left unchecked. The response to this "threat" was a discourse of "moral panic" which Hazel Carby examines in "Policing the Black Woman's Body in an Urban Context." Significantly, the migrant black woman in the United States was constructed as inherently degenerate and a sexualized threat to social balance. Carby argues that by inciting a "moral panic" about the African American migrant woman as a social danger, the discourse sought to hold this new geographical mobility for black women in check.[8]

---

[8]   Among the texts that Carby considers in her article are two biographies of Josephine Baker: Baker's autobiography, *Josephine*, written with Jo Bouillon, and Phyllis Rose's *Jazz Cleopatra*. She cites the narrative of Baker's early life (as it is described in both books) as an example of resistance to the kind of policing described above. Baker's hiring by a touring entertainment group, the Dixie Steppers, in her teens, offered an escape from the abysmally low-paying cleaning jobs she endured throughout adolescence and presented an opportunity for movement into the urban landscape. Yet the escape produced a kind of double-bind, as "the dance hall and the cabaret" were the "most frequently referenced landscapes in which black female promiscuity and sexual degeneracy were described" within this discourse (Carby 752). Though Carby does not cite them in her article, two anecdotes culled from Baker's composite biography reveal this construction of black female sexuality as a social menace. In *Jazz Cleopatra*, Phyllis Rose writes that Baker lost an early job as a live-in housekeeper for a couple named the Masons "when Mr. Mason began showing an interest in her" (13). Similarly, in *Remembering Josephine*, Stephen Papich hints that Baker's sexual appeal burdened an early professional relationship with the famous blues singer, Bessie Smith. Baker's hiring to serve as the singer's cleaning woman is reported (presumably through Baker's memory) as having carried Smith's proviso: "No drinkin', no smokin' dope, and no fuckin' the musicians" (30). Papich later writes that some sources explain Baker's and Smith's eventual parting as

Both of these contexts – white specularity of the black female body and "moral panic" over the black woman's sexuality – are germane to a rereading of Baker's early performances. Baker played with these constructions in the context of her jungle scenarios; time and again she appeared onstage as a sexual beast that needed to be captured or contained. In her appearance as a dragonfly in the 1930–31 *Folies* she was outfitted in a primitivist variation of a conventional chorus girl outfit – short and sparkly, exposing her legs, but with large, diaphanous wings. As the scene unfolded, Baker was chased by hunters who tried to sever her wings, eventually doing so by the scene's finale. The tableau rehearsed both the emphasis of black female difference that Gilman documents and the discursive policing that Carby describes in her article: the scene shows white males surrounding the exotic and sexually enticing black female, eventually stripping her of her potential for mobility/flight.[9] Thus, Baker pushed the construction of herself as a sexual threat to exaggerated extremes, portraying herself as not just a moral peril but as a veritable danger in the jungle spectacle. Show business had allowed her a physical escape from East St. Louis and offered an outlet through which she could illustrate the absurdity of the discourses that had tried to contain her. For Baker, performance was not a frivolous undertaking but the enterprise through which she might articulate meaningful social criticism.

Indeed, historical studies of African American culture suggest that within the black American vernacular tradition, the ostensible frivolity of musical performance may belie socially-pointed parody or political commentary. Both Lawrence Levine and William Pierson, for example, have written about the satirical function of African American dance and music. In *Black Culture and Consciousness*, Levine cites eighteenth- and nineteenth-century African American slaves parodying the behavior of their white masters through music and dance in ways that were often lost on white spectators. As one slave recalled:

> Us slaves watched white folks' parties where the guests danced a minuet and then paraded in a grand march, with the ladies and gentleman going different ways and then meeting again, arm in arm, and marching down the center together. Then we'd do it, too, *but we used to mock 'em*, every step. Sometimes the white folks noticed it, but they seemed to like it; I guess they thought we couldn't dance any better. (qtd. in Levine 17)

In *Black Legacy*, Pierson cites a recollection of Tennessee slaves doing the cakewalk:

---

occurring because "Bessie's boyfriend was getting too close [to Baker] and making too obvious advances" (38).

9   In the 1934 film *Zou Zou*, Baker's first talkie, she dramatized this containment once more. The film's centerpiece is Baker's performance of the song "Haiti" – a scene that sees her in diaphanous wings again, swinging from a perch in an oversized cage.

> The slaves both young and old would dress up in hand-me-down finery to do a high-kicking, prancing walk-around. They did a take-off on the high manners of the white folks in the "big house," but their masters, who gathered around to watch the fun, missed the point. (qtd in Pierson 64)

This parody through dance was to endure into the twentieth century and continue amidst the emergence of modern jazz dance out of the African American folk tradition. Karen Blackstein notes, for example, that at its origins the Charleston – Josephine Baker's signature step – not only "Africanized" and reconceptualized the European quadrille, but also "mocked the prancing of the white masters who danced those quadrilles" (242).

The doubleness on which this satire turns provides the starting point for many studies of African American culture. These investigations posit that black America wears two faces by necessity: a carefully accommodating mask donned before its white oppressors and the "genuine" persona that it adopts when that menace is absent. The tension between the doubleness naturalizes performance in everyday life for African Americans who must be constantly aware of white spectatorship. As W.E.B. Du Bois has written: "It is a peculiar sensation, this double-consciousness, this sense of always looking at one's self through the eyes of others, of measuring one's soul by the tape of a world that looks on in amused contempt and pity" (215).[10] More recently, African American theorist Henry Louis Gates, Jr., has argued that the naturalized performance of "double-consciousness" is reflected and embodied in signifyin(g), a rhetorical strategy of the African American literary tradition, through which the duality is negotiated (1984: 285).[11] Gates thus builds upon Du Bois' argument and notes the ubiquity of doubleness in the African American arts:

> Free of the white person's gaze, black people created their own unique vernacular structures and relished in the double play that these forms bore to white

---

[10] Similarly, in the preface to *Black Culture and Black Consciousness*, Lawrence Levine notes a song "sung by generations of Negroes" which summarizes the phenomenon as well:
> Got one mind for white folks to see,
> 'Nother for what I know is me;
> He don't know, he don't know my mind (xiii).

Frantz Fanon begins *Black Skin, White Masks* with a similar notion, noting the prevalence of this divided character among colonized blacks throughout the world:
> The black man has two dimensions. One with his fellows, the other with the white man. A Negro behaves differently with a white man and with another Negro. That this self-division is a direct result of colonialist subjugation is beyond question.... (17)

[11] Gates brackets the final 'g' of the term to simulate the aurality of the word's pronunciation within the black American argot and thus plays with the negotiation he is charting between spoken and written texts.

forms. Repetition and revision are fundamental to black artistic forms, from painting and sculpture to music and language use. (1988: xxiv)[12]

Signifyin(g) is a "structure of performance" that Gates posits can "apply equally to verbal texts and musical texts" (1988: 69). The examples noted above (and the well-documented inseparability of dance and music within African American culture) suggest that dance may fit within the "structure of performance" Gates is charting.[13] They reveal dance as a manifestation of the parodic aspect of signifyin(g): a negotiation of doubleness through parodic movement and exaggerated

---

[12]   However, Gates' contemporary Houston Baker has complicated this reading of double-consciousness as a simple duality. Baker posits that to see double-consciousness as merely a Janus-like state – a clean split of African American subjectivity into two dissimilar faces – is reductive. To assume that white spectatorship alone is the impetus for a neat division of black consciousness, between an essential character and a mask donned for whites, is to re-hearse what Baker sees as an "overdetermined" dualism of self-and-other (1985: 382). In his own writing on African American literature, Baker theorizes black consciousness as a tri-pling: the rent between a black vernacular self and the identity assumed in the face of inter-action with whites, plus the addition of a superlevel of consciousness that is aware of these "selves" and tries to negotiate their separation. As Baker writes, the challenge of the African American cultural performer is to "transform an obscene situation, a tripled metastatus, into a signal self/cultural expression" (1985, 393). In her essay, "In the Kingdom of Culture," Darlene Clark Hine complicates Du Bois' binary as well, arguing that if Du Bois had "con-sidered the issue of gender … he would have mused about how one ever feels her 'fiveness': Negro, American, woman, poor, black woman" (338). Thus, it is worth noting here that I do not see Du Bois' explication of black consciousness as a duality as an ascendant truth, but rather as a construct through which the reception of Baker's performances might be reread. In this way, I comply with Bernard Bell's assertion that the Du Boisian notion of double-consciousness is a rhetorical move that announces possibility. As Bell writes, "Rather than a sociocultural conflict that has been inevitably internalized as incipient personal pathology, African American double consciousness thus signifies a biracial, bicultural state of being in the world, an existential site of socialized cultural ambivalence and *emancipatory possibilities of personal and social transformation, and a dynamic epistemological mode of critical inquiry for African Americans* (96, my emphasis).

[13]   On the inseparability of music and dance in African American culture, see *Steppin' on the Blues: The Visible Rhythms of African American Dance* by Jacqui Malone and *Jookin': The Rise of Social Dance Formations in African-American Culture* by Katrina Hazzard-Gordon. Malone writes, for example:

A tendency to "dance the song" in traditional African cultures was preserved in the secular and sacred expression of U.S. slaves.… To thoroughly understand … slave songs one must imagine them as performed. For they were not just sung at worship services and in the field but they were also danced in the ring shout. (28–29)

Similarly, in a 1931 article for the *Cleveland News* based on interviews with Duke Ellington, Archie Bell wrote

When [Ellington] is composing he doesn't ask himself whether he is putting down notes that will be admired and praised by conservatory professors of theory, harmony and composition: "Will that musical phrase give 'em a kick?" or "will they feel like hopping around a bit when they hear that?" (53)

exhibition – that device I read in Josephine Baker's performances – always "repeating and simultaneously reversing [received racist images] in one deft, discursive act" (Gates 1985, 286).

In the two accounts from Levine and Pierson above, the parodist plays upon the white audience's misconception that the awkwardness of the dancing marks a failure for the black performer to emulate the "innate" grace of whites. Rather, the performer's movements instead exaggerate white sophistication itself as affected instead of inherent. Baker's primitive performances in twentieth century Paris built on this tradition – varying, though, in the way they parodied the conventions of racialized hierarchization not from the "top down" but from the "bottom up." Just as slaves were wont to satirize the pomp of their masters and reveal the illegitimacy of the genetic superiority that whites were so quick to assume for themselves, Baker's parodic dances exposed the error of the converse assumption in the schema: that blacks were inherently inferior primitives.

Baker's parody of racial essentialism in the 1920s and 1930s can be read through Judith Butler's theory of parody in the performance of drag, which she argues is a challenge to received notions of essential gender traits, rather than a mere impersonation. As Butler writes in *Gender Trouble*, what we perceive to be conventionally male or female behavior is not a projection of essential biological difference, but rather a dramatization of discursive impositions that announce: this is how men or women are.

> In other words, acts, gestures and desire produce the effect of an internalized core or substance, but produce this *on the surface* of the body…. Such acts, gestures, enactments, generally construed, are *performative* in the sense that the essence or identity that they otherwise purport to express are *fabrications* manufactured and sustained through corporeal signs and other discursive means. (136)

Thus, Butler continues, "the notion of an original or primary gender identity is often parodied within the cultural practices of drag, cross-dressing, and the sexual stylization of butch-femme identities…. *In imitating gender, drag implicitly reveals the imitative structure of gender itself*" (137). The performance of drag does not entail an imitation of opposite gender identity; it reveals how gender is itself performative, a role played from an exterior script. Similarly, Baker challenged the veracity of primitivist conventions by pushing them into absurdity and exposing their essentially contrived nature. Baker's performances disputed the construct of an African American essence by overstating the effects of that assumed essence on the body's exterior. For instance, the exaggeration of her monkey's walk and savage dance were overwrought dramatizations of how blacks were believed to behave. Her animal-like movements exposed the necessary performance that blacks had assumed, revealing the Negro's supposed animalism as an ongoing act that had been proscribed by whites. Baker performed performance; hers was an act that intended its affectation to be conspicuous.

The move required that she adopt an "accommodating" guise at times. Superficially, Baker may have appeared in her performances to be acquiescing to racist conventions with minimal resistance. However, Baker's utilization of the animal/primitive stereotype was a deceptively clever parody that spoke concession while it whispered rebuttal. Just as African American slaves signified on the received notion that they were graceless and unrefined with their exaggerated waltzes and stilted quadrilles, Baker played with the white misconception that blacks were, by their very essence, naturally primitive and less civilized. The ruse was a tough negotiation. Like the minstrel and vaudeville performances that preceded it, it required the apparent confirmation of distorted representations while allowing room for the exhibition of distance between the performer's "actual self" and those same ill-conceived notions. The more outlandishly distorted the performer's stage persona was, then, the more the entertainer might challenge the received stereotype. The minstrel performers' strategy was to affirm and exaggerate injurious representations of blacks that had been implemented by whites and then contradict the notions by discarding the grotesque affectation offstage. They intended to perpetuate uncertainty about stereotypes through the discrepancy.[14] However, this strategy sometimes collapsed against the peril of preconceived white reception. The connectedness of black performativity and white racist ideologies in the formation of the minstrel show's conventions complicated the attempts at resistance among black minstrel performers. As Eric Lott writes in his comprehensive study of blackface minstrelsy, *Love and Theft*:

> Black performance itself, first of all, was precisely "performative," a cultural invention, not some precious essence installed in black bodies; and for better or worse it was often a product of self-commodification, a way of getting along in a constricted world. Black people, that is to say, not only exercised a certain amount of control over such practices but perforce sometimes developed them in tandem with white spectators. Moreover, practices taken as black were

---

[14] There were precedents for the formula. In the vaudeville shows of the early twentieth century, other African American performers had struggled to maintain that same balance. As Nathan Huggins writes:

> Black men ... could use the theatrical grotesques as ways of marking distance between themselves and their horror. But since these were racial delineations – white fantasy's conscription of black men to serve its needs – the problem of maintaining distance for the Negro was crucial and difficult. Bert Williams and George Walker ... tried to use the stereotype as an instrumental satire.... When this team billed themselves as "Two Real Coons," they were not portraying themselves or any other Negroes they knew.... Some black performers attempted to achieve the distance between the stage characters and themselves by the very extremities of the exaggeration. (257–58)

occasionally interracial creations whose commodification on white stages attested only to whites' greater access to public distribution (and profit). (39)

Ultimately, as Lott concludes, the commodified and deformed version of black performativity presented by the white minstrel performers who dominated the entertainment was confused for an authentic and essential "blackness" by white audiences. Too often blackface minstrelsy was received as the exhibition of black cultural practice rather than the performance of racialized exaggerations.

In the face of this potential threat, Baker modified the strategy of juxtaposition employed by black minstrel performers. Here I return to the suggestion that Baker intentionally constructed her offstage visage as the antithesis of the primitive guise she repeatedly assumed onstage. In addition, though, Baker fit the calculated incongruity between her two sides *into* her act to maximize its exposure. In this way she worked to prevent the type of audience misreadings that Lott documents. Though Baker's early shows are best remembered for their recurring evocation of the primitive, at times they presented her in a glamorous, refined setting as well – a juxtaposition that had startling effects. Phyllis Rose notes, for example, the potent response elicited by Baker's glamorous emergence in a scene from a 1928 show that immediately followed a tableau in which she performed in rags:

> She went offstage and reappeared in – a dress! A well-cut elegant dress, such as she wore for her nightclub performances but not onstage. Her tight-fitting cloche of rhinestones shone in the spotlight…. Everyone understood. Look how much progress she has made, they said. Look how assimilated she has become, how domesticated, how civilized. (122)

Baker was signifying on the assumed boundaries forged by racial essentialism.

Furthermore, though Baker's performances and physical presentation repeatedly parodied the way white discourse had represented the Negro in general, her work also challenged tropes in the more specific constructions of black female sexuality. For one, her onstage dancing style ridiculed and toyed with the persistent white tendency, noted by Sander Gilman, to view the black woman's body as a series of alien parts rather than as a unified whole. In her essay, "Selling Hot Pussy: Representations of Black Female Sexuality in the Cultural Marketplace," bell hooks locates the French fascination with Baker's nearly-nude performances in a continuum with the earlier European representations of black female sexuality that Gilman documents. Baker's dancing, which frequently featured the exaggerated movement of her behind, was an exploitation of the enduring white eroticization of the black body (hooks 63). Hooks quotes from Phyllis Rose to formulate the argument and detail how Baker overturned the Victorian conventions that had inscribed the black woman's behind as an icon of grotesque, aberrant sexuality:

> One can hardly overemphasize the importance of her rear end. Baker herself declared that people had been hiding their asses for too long. "The rear end exists. I see no reason to be ashamed of it. It's true there are rear ends so stupid, so pretentious, so insignificant that they're good only for sitting on." With Baker's triumph, the erotic gaze of a nation moved downward: she had uncovered a new region for desire (Rose qtd. in hooks 24).

Thus, her dancing style denounced and reconfigured Europeans' earlier tendency to view the black female body in parts. As Ann Douglas writes, the jazz dances that Baker made popular emphasized not only "the patterned movement of feet in regular time, but the entire body's lively interpretation of an often surprising beat" (52). This form of dancing depended on the participant's ability to control various parts of the body at once. It built on the West African tradition, in which the "dancer may pick up and respond to the rhythms of one or more drums, depending on his skill, [and] in the best dancing ... [add] another rhythm, one that is not there. He tunes his ear to hidden rhythms, and he dances to gaps in the music" (Chernoff 144). The Hottentot Venus had been made to stand still in static exhibition, allowing for the slow dissection of her body under the white gaze. Baker's performances, on the contrary, showcased certain body parts while commanding notice of the entire mobile design. They challenged the spectator to observe her various parts as they moved to a variety of rhythms. Her wondrous motion defied a thorough inspection.

Baker also challenged constructions of black female sexuality through androgyny. She frequently stimulated racial anxieties, obscuring the boundary between black "female" temptation and "male" danger by throwing this gendered division into disarray. The banana skirt, for example, her most famous costume, seemed at times an intentionally absurd signifier of the black male phallic threat that Fanon describes in *Black Skin, White Masks*: "The white man is convinced that the Negro is a beast; if it is not the length of the penis, then it is the sexual potency that impresses him" (170). As the costume evolved, Baker's phallic signifier became less playful and more menacing. The outfit's incarnation in the 1927 *Folies* show was "a spangled, hard-edged version. It was the fate of those bananas to become ever harder and more threatening with the years, so that at last they looked like spikes" (Rose 114). This play could have particularly disruptive effects within certain contexts – such as Baker's various late-1920s performances in Germany. As Nancy Nenno points out, in the wake of that country's 1920 occupation by French African troops – a period that came to be called "Schwarze Schmach am Rhein," the "Black Humiliation on the Rhine" – German newspapers repeatedly cast the occupation in the rhetoric of sexual invasion, constructing "the African soldiers as animals who, possessed by an excessive and perverse sexual drive, threatened modern Europe with their jungle mentality" (152).[15] Baker's spiky phalluses could be interpreted as an unnerving signifier that might recall German anxiety over the presence of black men in the Rhineland.

At other times, Baker's juxtaposition of gender signifiers in performance was more complex – androgyny exaggerated to bewildering extremes. The *Candide* review of her inaugural *Revue Nègre* performance documents this: "At one point a strange figure in a ragged undershirt ambles onto the stage.... Josephine Baker. Woman or man? Her lips are painted black, her skin is the color of bananas, her cropped hair sticks to her head like caviar, her voice squeaks" (qtd. in Baker and Bouillon 55). Phyllis Rose reports that Baker's squeaky voice perpetuated the ambiguity; some observers of that performance thought that she sang like a man (25). In her 1932 show at the Casino de Paris she appeared as one, dressed in a top hat and tails to play a bandleader in one of the program's scenes. The performance marked a complete transformation from her initial appearances on the Paris stage: the figure who had first appeared as a topless savage woman had evolved into a lighter-skinned, well-dressed man. The stereotypical Other had assumed its oppressor's face.

Baker's fluidity on and offstage was the vehicle through which she consistently parodied a wide range of oppressive constructions of "blackness" in the 1920s and 1930s. Her work thrived on subversive repetition, on the appropriation of stereotypes and their reconfiguration. The combination of ostensible acquiescence and endorsement of black difference that she crafted in her stage appearances mark her as a signal player in the cultural performance of African American modernism. She was a master of what Houston Baker identifies in *Modernism and the Harlem Renaissance* as the two guiding tropes of black modernist art and literature: the *mastery of form* and the *deformation of mastery*. Baker likens both concepts to the wearing of masks. Mastery of form is the assumption of a minstrel-type mask, a mask that conceals "real" black identity, through which the African American cultural performer may speak to whites from a position of safety (15–17). On the other hand, deformation of mastery is the donning of a mask that distinguishes, that *advertises* black difference as through vernacular performance (49–51).[16] Both of these masks figured prominently in Josephine Baker's strategic performance. If, as Houston Baker argues, a successful mastery of form entails an understanding of "the game" of minstrelsy – a form "designed to remind white consciousness that black men and women are *misspeakers* bereft of humanity" – then surely her deft turns on existing conventions

---

[15] Nenno's article, "Femininity, the Primitive, and Modern Urban Space: Josephine Baker in Berlin," offers a more detailed exploration of Baker's performances in 1920s Germany.

[16] In defining mastery of form and deformation of mastery, Baker suggests that the Ur-texts for these two modes of cultural performance are Booker T. Washington's assumption of the minstrel mask in his famous "Atlanta Compromise" address of 1895 and W.E.B. Du Bois' vernacular-influenced *The Souls of Black Folk*, respectively.

in minstrel entertainment qualify her as a veritable master of mastery (1987: 21). Likewise, if deformation is a "go(uer)illa action in the face of acknowledged adversaries" – with all the jungle resonances appropriate to Josephine Baker's stage presence – that requires the display of decidedly black alternatives to the "non-sense" of the minstrel mask, then there are few better examples of the mode than her dancing, rooted so soundly in the music and rhythmic sense of African American tradition (1987: 50).[17] Fluidly exploring the range of possibilities between these two modes, Baker contested the complex of representations that had oppressed blacks for so long.

Later, as her career progressed and she accumulated wealth and influence, she challenged discursive and material restraints in other ways, by "combining performance with civil rights activism" (Rose 212). In 1951, for example, she "was the first black headliner to succeed in getting her whole troupe housed at the hotel where they were working" rather than at some designated "Negro" accommodation in another part of town (Rose 212).[18] Yet the trajectory of her career need not be read as an early selling-out that allowed for the agency that followed. Baker's early performances are rich with satire and deft in their play with contemporary cultural contexts. "It is the intelligence of my body that I have exploited," she was once quoted as saying (O'Connor 90), and it was that self-named intelligence that "allowed her at times to transcend the gilded cage of her situation" (Rony 203). Baker kept audiences guessing about, and grasping for, the certainty of accepted stereotypes. Incessantly elusive, she was the slippery signifier in the racial and sexual spectacles of Jazz Age popular culture.

Works Cited

Baker, Houston. "Caliban's Triple Play." "Race," Writing and Difference. Ed. Henry Louis Gates, Jr. Chicago: U of Chicago P, 1985. 381–95.
—. Modernism and the Harlem Renaissance. Chicago: U of Chicago P, 1987.
Baker, Josephine, actor. Zou Zou. Dir. Marc Allegret. With Jean Gabin. Production Arys, 1934.
—. and Jo Bouillon. Josephine. Trans. Mariana Fitzpatrick. New York: Harper and Row, 1977.

---

[17] Baker intends the uneasy punning about the jungle and African American traditions. He plays with idea of "go(uer)rilla" action as being a necessary defense against the infiltration of (white) "Man–the master of 'civilization'" who "triggers [this] response" (1987: 50).

[18] For a more complete account of Baker's civil rights activism after the Second World War, see Rose 212–15.

Bell, Archie. "Duke Ellington's Orchestra Draws Big Crowds." *The Duke Ellington Reader.* Ed. Mark Tucker. New York: Oxford UP, 1993. 52–4.

Bell, Bernard W. "Genealogical Shifts in Du Bois's Discourse on Double Consciousness as the Sign of African American Difference." *W.E.B. Du Bois on Race and Culture: Philosophy, Politics, and Poetics.* Ed. Bernard W. Bell, et al. New York: Routledge, 1996. 87–108.

Bhabha, Homi K. *The Location of Culture.* London: Routledge, 1994.

Blackstein, Karen. "Keeping the Spirit Alive: The Jazz Dance Testament of Mura Dehn." *Representing Jazz.* Ed. Krin Gabbard. Durham: Duke UP, 1995. 229–46.

Butler, Judith. *Gender Trouble: Feminism and the Subversion of Identity.* New York: Routledge, 1990.

Carby, Hazel. "Policing the Black Woman's Body in an Urban Context." *Critical Inquiry* 18.4 (1992): 738–55.

Chernoff, John Miller. *African Rhythm and African Sensibility: Aesthetics and Social Action in African Musical Idioms.* Chicago: U of Chicago P, 1979.

Dalton, Karen C. C., and Henry Louis Gates, Jr. "Josephine Baker and Paul Colin: African American Dance Seen through Parisian Eyes." *Critical Inquiry* 24.4 (1998): 903–934.

Douglas, Ann. *Terrible Honesty: Mongrel Manhattan in the 1920s.* New York: Farrar, Straus and Giroux, 1995.

Du Bois, W.E.B. *The Souls of Black Folk. Three Negro Classics.* Introd. by John Hope Franklin. New York: Avon, 1965. 207–390.

Dyer, Richard. *The Matter of Images: Essays on Representations.* London: Routledge, 1993.

Fanon, Frantz. *Black Skins, White Masks.* Trans. Charles Lam Markmann. New York: Grove, 1967.

Flanner, Janet. *Paris Was Yesterday: 1925–1939.* Ed. Irving Drutman. New York: Viking, 1972.

Floyd, Samuel A., Jr. "Music in the Harlem Renaissance: An Overview." *Black Music in the Harlem Renaissance: A Collection of Essays.* Contributions in Afro-American and African Studies, Number 128. Ed. Samuel A. Floyd, Jr. Westport, CT: Greenwood P, 1990. 1–27.

Gates, Henry Louis, Jr. "The Blackness of Blackness: A Critique of the Sign and the Signifying Monkey." *Black Literature and Literary Theory.* Ed. Henry Louis Gates, Jr. New York: Routledge, 1984. 223–611.

—.   "An Interview with Josephine Baker and James Baldwin, with an Introduction by Anthony Barthelemy." *Southern Review* 21.3 (1985): 594–602.

—.   *The Signifying Monkey: A Theory of African-American Literary Criticism.* New York: Oxford UP, 1988.

Gilman, Sander L. "Black Bodies, White Bodies: Toward an Iconography of Female Sexuality in Late Nineteenth-Century Art, Medicine, and

Literature." *"Race," Writing and Difference.* Ed. Henry Louis Gates, Jr. Chicago: U of Chicago P, 1985. 204–42.

Hazzard-Gordon, Katrina. *Jookin': The Rise of Social Dance Formations in African-American Culture.* Philadelphia: Temple UP, 1990.

Hine, Darlene Clark. "In the Kingdom of Culture: Black Women and the Intersection of Race, Gender, and Class." *Lure and Loathing: Essays on Race, Identity, and the Ambivalence of Assimilation.* Ed. Gerald Early. New York: Penguin, 1993.

hooks, bell. *Black Looks: Race and Representation.* Toronto: Between the Lines, 1992.

Huggins, Nathan Irvin. *Harlem Renaissance.* New York: Oxford UP, 1971.

Levine, Lawrence. *Black Culture and Black Consciousness: Afro-American Thought from Slavery to Freedom.* New York: Oxford UP, 1977.

Locke, Alain. "The New Negro." *The New Negro: An Interpretation.* Ed. Alain Locke. New York: Albert and Charles Boni, 1925. 3–16.

Lott, Eric. *Love and Theft: Blackface Minstrelsy and the American Working Class.* New York: Oxford UP, 1993.

Malone, Jacqui. *Steppin' on the Blues: The Visible Rhythms of African American Dance.* Urbana: U of Illinois P, 1996.

Martin, Wendy. "'Remembering the Jungle': Josephine Baker and Modernist Parody." *Prehistories of the Future: The Primitivist Project and the Culture of Modernism.* Ed. Elazar Barkan and Ronald Bush. Stanford: Stanford UP, 1995. 310–325.

McClintock, Anne. *Imperial Leather: Race, Gender and Sexuality in the Colonial Contest.* New York: Routledge, 1995.

Nenno, Nancy. "Femininity, the Primitive, and Modern Urban Space: Josephine Baker in Berlin." *Women in the Metropolis: Gender and Modernity in the Weimar Culture.* Ed. Katharina von Ankum. Berkeley: U of California P, 1997. 145–161.

O'Connor, Patrick. *Josephine Baker.* Boston: Little, Brown, 1988.

Papich, Stephen. *Remembering Josephine.* New York: Bobbs-Merrill, 1976.

Pierson, William D. *Black Legacy: America's Hidden Heritage.* Amherst: U of Massachusetts P, 1993.

Rony, Fatimah Tobing. *The Third Eye: Race, Cinema, and Ethnographic Spectacle.* Durham: Duke UP, 1996.

Rose, Phyllis. *Jazz Cleopatra: Josephine Baker In Her Time.* New York: Doubleday, 1989.

Tucker, Mark, ed. *The Duke Ellington Reader.* New York: Oxford UP, 1993.

Williams, Patricia. *The Alchemy of Race and Rights.* Cambridge: Harvard UP, 1991.

Re-scripting Origins:
Zora Neale Hurston's Staging of Black Vernacular Dance

Anthea Kraut

Canonization and Obscurity:
Zora Neale Hurston's Place in the Academy

Over the last two decades, the study of Zora Neale Hurston has flourished, with her 1937 novel *Their Eyes Were Watching God* in particular earning a place in multiple literary traditions, including the American, black, and feminist canons.[1] By and large, scholars celebrate Hurston for her ability to adapt non-literate folk traditions to literary forms and for embracing the black vernacular culture of the rural South; academia has so lionized Hurston, in fact, that scholar Ann duCille coins the term "Hurstonism" to describe the critical construction of her as the quintessential signifier of the folk and the foremother of a black women's literary tradition. Yet even amidst this resurgence of attention, Hurston's contributions to the field of American dance have remained largely obscured. Remarkably few scholars have noted that, in the 1930s, Hurston assembled a group of sixteen Bahamian dancers and rehearsed, directed, produced, and performed in a series of concerts consisting of folksongs, dances, and pantomime. The material for these performances arose directly from Hurston's anthropological research in the southern United States and the Bahamas as well as out of her desire to communicate black cultural forms to a broad public. Hurston's first revue, *The Great Day*, which premiered on Broadway in January of 1932, was arranged around a single day in the life of a railroad work camp, from daybreak until dusk, with a West Indian fire dance serving as the climactic finale. Over the next few years, Hurston continued her attempts to produce this folk concert, presenting it in slightly different versions and under various titles – *From Sun to Sun, Singing Steel, All De Live Long Day* – in cities across the country, including Chicago, St. Louis, Washington D.C., and Winter Park, Florida. Al-

---

[1] I am extremely grateful to Professor Susan Manning, whose insightful criticism and continual guidance have been invaluable to my work, and to Marta Effinger, whose input was instrumental early on in the writing of this essay. I also wish to acknowledge the support of a Northwestern University Dissertation Grant and an American Society for Theatre Research Fellowship, which made possible my archival research in the summer of 1999. An earlier version of this paper was presented at the Black Theatre Network Conference in Winston-Salem, North Carolina, 1999.

though Hurston continually re-worked the concert, inserting and removing certain scenes, the enactment of the Caribbean folk dance remained a fixture that
was, by all accounts, the high point of the production.

While further work is needed before the record of these revues can be fully
restored and evaluated, it is clear that dance was indeed a crucial component of
the "*real* Negro art theatre" that Hurston envisioned and attempted to institute.[2]
The question that immediately arises is how these revues – which were favorably
received by black and white critics alike – have so eluded the notice of dance
historians. In *The Black Tradition in American Dance,* Richard Long does make
brief mention of Hurston's *The Great Day* concert in a section titled "The Bahamian Connection" (40–41). But neither Lynn Fauley Emery's canonical *Black
Dance from 1619 to Today,* which does refer to Hurston's written analysis of
dance, nor John O. Perpener, III's *The Seminal Years of Black Concert Dance*
includes any account of Hurston's theatrical productions. These and other
histories of African American concert dance, including essays by Joe Nash and
William Moore in Gerald Myers's *The Black Tradition in American Modern Dance,*
focus their attention on a number of Hurston's contemporaries in the field of
dance – figures such as Hemsley Winfield, Edna Guy, Asadata Dafora, Alison
Boroughs, Charles Williams, and, most prominently, Katherine Dunham and
Pearl Primus, "the two true pioneers of Black concert dance" (Moore 15). And
while scholars like Brenda Dixon-Stowell,[3] Zita Allen, and Susan Manning have
elucidated the inherent problems and pitfalls of designating a separate "black
dance" tradition, there is little question that the formation of a black concert
dance tradition was propelled in the 1930s by stage presentations of the roots of
African American dance. First produced a full two years prior to Dafora's
celebrated *Kykunkor* and five years prior to the momentous *Negro Dance Evening,*
two dance events which assume conspicuous positions in existing historical accounts, Hurston's folk revue – with its ostensibly "authentic" West Indian dance
number – certainly qualifies for inclusion in genealogies of black concert dance.[4]

---

2 See Hurston, "Letter to Langston Hughes," 12 Apr. 1928.
3 Now Brenda Dixon Gottschild
4 Significantly, Joe Nash's delineation of the "Pioneers in Negro Concert Dance" between
   1931 and 1937 places Hall Johnson's 1933 Broadway success *Run Little Chillun* on the map of
   black concert dance's early years. Although the dances in this production were officially, as
   Nash records, staged by famed white modern dance choreographer Doris Humphrey, by all
   indications, it was Hurston's troupe of Bahamian dancers as well as Hurston's choreography
   that were featured in Johnson's program. See Hurston's *Dust Tracks on a Road* for her comments on the uncanny resemblance between her own Bahamian number and the one in *Run
   Little Chillun* (284). A letter from Alain Locke to Charlotte Osgood Mason, Hurston's patron,
   suggests that Johnson was, in fact, guilt-ridden over his "theft" of Hurston's dancers; Locke,
   "Letter to Mason," 18 Apr. 1933.

Although any attempts to explain Hurston's absence from dance history must remain conjectural, several possible explanations exist. To start with, given that Hurston's literary work was only recovered from obscurity in the late 1970s, it is perhaps not surprising that her far more ephemeral choreographic work also has escaped widespread notice.[5] As Barbara Speisman explains with regard to Hurston's theatrical career in general, "Perhaps one of the chief reasons her plays have not received the attention they deserve is that so few of her manuscripts are in published form" (34). Similarly, it is worth recalling that Hurston's chapter "Concert," which details her theatrical efforts, was not accessible to the public until 1995, when Cheryl Wall and the Library of America published the restored text of Hurston's 1942 autobiography, *Dust Tracks on a Road*, in *Folklore, Memoirs, and Other Writings*.[6] To echo scholar Lynda Hill, the availability of this kind of documentation is "essential ... to be able to write a thorough historical account" of Hurston's staged productions and thus of her choreography as well (201).

But a confluence of historical factors may also be responsible for impeding greater recognition of Hurston's dance praxis. In order to shed light on these historical conditions, we must first situate Hurston in relation to the Harlem Renaissance, for while she is customarily identified with the flourishing of African American cultural production in the 1920s, her relationship to many Renaissance figures was uneasy at best (Hemenway 64–65). As Hemenway points out, Hurston's autobiography contains only passing mention of the New Negro movement (35). Many of the Harlem literati, moreover, mistook Hurston's interest in performance as a lack of serious intellectual commitment.[7] Hurston's relationship with Langston Hughes in particular was especially fraught, for although the two shared the patronage of Charlotte Osgood Mason, as well as an enthusiasm for establishing a theatre based on African American folk practices, their failed collaboration on the play *Mule Bone* in 1930 produced a rift between the two that was never healed.[8] This split assumes greater importance for dance

---

[5] Renewed attention to Hurston's literature was launched by the recuperative work of Robert Hemenway and Alice Walker in the 1970s.

[6] As Cheryl Wall notes in her edited volume of Hurston's *Folklore, Memoirs, and Other Writings*, the title page of the *Dust Tracks* manuscript contains a handwritten note that reads, "Parts of this manuscript were not used in the final composition of the book for publisher's reasons" (982).

[7] See, for example, Hughes's reference to Hurston as a "perfect book of entertainment" in his autobiography, *The Big Sea* (qtd. in Hemenway 64). Lynda Hill speculates that it was Hurston's commitment to the theatre that may have resulted in her contemporaries' emphasis on her "stagelike persona" over and above her serious intellectual pursuits (xxiii).

[8] See Langston Hughes and Zora Neale Hurston, *Mule Bone: A Comedy of Negro Life*. Rachel Rosenberg's "Looking for Zora's *Mule Bone*" provides an excellent analysis of the conflict between Hurston and Hughes. See also Ruthe T. Sheffey on the collaboration between the two.

history when we consider Hughes's 1967 book *Black Magic*, a pictorial history of African Americans in the performing arts, which he co-authored with Milton Meltzer. In a chapter on "Dancers and Dancing," Hughes traces a history of black dance on the concert stage that credits Dafora's *Kykunkor* with first bringing the interpretation of African-derived dance to public attention, appoints Katherine Dunham as "the most distinguished pioneer in the transition of folk and popular dances from the ethnic into the interpretive" (266), cites Hemsley Winfield, Eugene Von Grona, and Pearl Primus – but nowhere mentions Hurston. Predating Emery's *Black Dance* by five years, the parallels between Hughes's chronicle – which does in fact serve as an important secondary source for Emery – and later histories are evident. While I do not mean to suggest that Hughes alone determined the course of African American dance historiography, I do think it is important to acknowledge the ways in which extant accounts influence subsequent ones, the ways that the scripting of history inevitably involves the re-writing of earlier narratives. And while we can only speculate about whether or not Hughes would have included Hurston's contributions to the field of dance had they remained friends, it seems likely that he was cognizant of her folk concerts and chose not to document them. What is certain is that once Hurston's choreographic endeavors were written out of dance history, it was all too easy for further work to perpetuate this erasure.

It is also worth considering the complicated and rather vexed relationship of dance to the New Negro Movement in general. While it may have seemed, as Hughes proclaims, as if "all Harlem was dancing" in the 1920s (91), for the Harlem Renaissance artist, "dance served primarily as a symbol of the times" (Perpener 26). The figure of the dancing black female in particular, several scholars have demonstrated, served as a recurrent referent in the period's discourses of primitivism, cropping up repeatedly in the writing of men like Hughes, Jean Toomer, and Claude McKay.[9] Yet the popular black dance styles that dominated the rent parties, nightclubs, cabarets, and musical theatre stages were considered too disreputable to count as "serious" artistic expression. So even while vaudeville and musical theatre stars like Josephine Baker, Bill "Bojangles" Robinson, and Florence Mills were widely admired, such performers were deemed in need of a "dignified medium," according to Alain Locke in a 1926 *Theatre Arts Monthly* article (qtd. in Stewart 81). "Perhaps," Perpener theorizes, "because dance, in its vernacular manifestations, represented what upper-class blacks considered the stereotypical image of their lower-class brothers, it was not held in high esteem as a theatrical art among the intelligentsia" (26–7).

---

[9]   The work of John Lowe, Nathan Huggins, and Barbara Christian all provide insight into the relationship between the image of the black female dancer and the trope of the primitive. For examples of such images, see Langston Hughes's "Jazzonia," reprinted in Locke's *The New Negro* (226), Jean Toomer's "Theater" in *Cane*, and Claude McKay's "Harlem Dancer."

With ambivalent feelings about dance's usefulness to the New Negro – about the ability of the form to combat racist assumptions and thus to effect social change – it is conceivable that Hurston's Harlem Renaissance contemporaries were hesitant to call attention to her choreographic endeavors.[10]

Finally, the fact that Hurston's concerts defy easy categorization may have aided in their disappearance from the historical record. Echoing the sentiments of Locke, African American dance artists of the 1920s and 30s like Hemsley Winfield and Edna Guy sought to differentiate their work from the "neo-minstrel stereotypes" of vaudeville and musical theatre and so increasingly drew distinctions between dance genres (Perpener 28). In large part, such divisions were based on performance locale, for these artists unmistakably drew on the vernacular forms of the black folk; yet like their literary counterparts in the Harlem Renaissance, they perceived these forms as "raw material" that could be re-cast into more acceptable modes only on the high art concert stage. And while Hurston likewise sought to distinguish her concerts from popular Broadway productions, a subject to which I will return shortly, she explicitly opposed the efforts of other African American performers to elevate the folk in the creation of an elite art. In a 1934 interview printed in the *Chicago Daily News*, for example, Hurston proclaims that "the Negro song as sung on the concert stage is a song with its face lifted"; her own program, in contrast, offers "songs sung as the unlettered Negroes sing them" (Hayes 27).[11] Such pronouncements, intended to differentiate her work from that of celebrated concert artists like Paul Robeson and Roland Hayes, may have also indirectly served to disassociate her work from the black concert dance tradition that was emerging in the 1930s. Accompanied by the fact that Hurston's revues featured vernacular dance alongside a range of expressive art forms, including work songs, spirituals, children's games, sermons, and comical skits, it is quite possible that Hurston's stagings fell between the cracks of dance history's generic boundaries.

More recently, two dissertations reverse this historical neglect of Hurston's dance endeavors: Leah Creque-Harris's *The Representation of African Dance on the Concert Stage: From the Early Black Musicals to Pearl Primus* and Elgie Gaynell Sherrod's *The Dance Griots: An Examination of the Dance Pedagogy of Katherine Dunham and Black Pioneering Dancers in Chicago and New York City, from 1931–1946.* Both reclaim Hurston as an important figure in the evolution of a black tradition in American dance, while designating *The Great Day* as "the first musical to present authentic African-based dance materials on a concert stage in

---

[10] In her autobiography, for example, Hurston reveals that Alain Locke initially opposed her concert plans (1996: 282).

[11] Indeed, Hurston expresses similar sentiments in her 1934 essay "Spirituals and Neo-Spirituals," in which she draws a distinction between "genuine Negro Spirituals" and the "concert artists and glee clubs" (Rpt. in 1981: 80).

America" (Sherrod 267). Like Creque-Harris and Sherrod, I want to submit Hurston's revues as inaugural events in the formation of a black concert dance movement – a movement spurred by stagings that highlighted the African roots of African American dance styles. At the same time, however, I hope to challenge standard accounts of black concert dance by revealing the very constructedness of this Afrocentric tradition, for, as accepted as it has become, the work of establishing such a tradition was neither seamless nor automatic. Yet the recovery of Hurston's dance undertakings has still further implications, prompting us not only to re-evaluate African American dance history but also to re-consider Hurston's relationship to the folk and their dance forms. In particular, as we begin to explore the complex workings of vernacular dance within Hurston's concerts, it is crucial that we strive to understand her artistic production as more than a direct continuation of black folk culture – a view that no doubt diminishes the careful and deliberate work she carried out in directing and producing these revues. Rather, the remainder of this essay will argue that Hurston subtly and skillfully transformed the expressive forms of the folk in an attempt to alter her audiences' understanding of black vernacular dance and its place in American history.[12]

Authenticity Claims and Critiques

There is no denying, however, that Hurston herself promoted her revues as "natural" representations of black folk life, thereby contributing to the discourse of folk authenticity that continues to surround her work. Writing about *The Great Day* in her autobiography, Hurston describes the concert's purpose: "to show what beauty and appeal there was in genuine Negro material, as against the Broadway concept" (1942, 158). Again and again, Hurston emphasized that hers was a "concert in the raw." A printed announcement for the revue, for

---

[12] Throughout this paper, I will use the word "folk" to indicate that group of people that Hurston persistently strove to represent in a multitude of genres – the unlettered class of African Americans residing in the rural South, as well as that same class of Caribbean peoples with whom her anthropological research put her in touch. To be sure, this particular formulation of the folk circulated extensively among many, but not all of Hurston's Harlem Renaissance contemporaries. Unlike Alain Locke, for example, Hurston regarded the folk as more than the mere producers of raw material in need of artistic refinement, insisting instead on exposing and exploring the integrity and roots of black folkloric traditions. I use the phrase "vernacular dance," meanwhile, to refer specifically to those communal dance practices and styles that emerge *apart* from theatrical, commercial settings. Understanding the vernacular in this way prompts us to explore the modifications and revisions that inevitably occur when vernacular forms are transformed into commodified cultural products such as theatrical stagings.

example, proclaims that "the spirituals used ... are fresh and without the artificial polish of re-arrangement," while a program note characterizes the concert as "a rare sample of the pure and unvarnished materials from which the stage and concert tradition has been derived" (Letter 15 Oct. 1931). And, as the words of reviewer Arthur Ruhl confirm, Hurston was largely successful in presenting her folk material as "unadulterated, and not fixed and fussed up for purposes of commerce" – in short, as "the real thing." "If there is such a thing as natural and unpremeditated art," Ruhl concludes, "here it seemed exemplified, by every one concerned" (11).

Despite such claims, I want to suggest that Hurston's assertions of authenticity are best understood as a *critique* of the kinds of representations of black vernacular styles that were prevalent in the early twentieth century – as her distinction between "genuine Negro material" and "the Broadway concept" should indicate. To be sure, Hurston was keenly aware of the effects of black musical theatre's success in the 1920s, especially in relation to white perceptions of the black dancing body. In an article titled "You Don't Know Us Negroes," written around 1934 for *American Mercury* but never published, Hurston contends that shows like Noble Sissle's and Eubie Blake's 1921 *Shuffle Along* "made a greater impression than is generally admitted." The power of this impression, she goes on to explain, derives from the fact that:

> most white people have seen our shows but not our lives. If they have not seen a Negro show they have seen a minstrel or at least a black-face comedian and that is considered enough. They know all about us. We say, "Am it?" And go into a dance. By way of catching breath we laugh and say, "Is you is, or is you ain't" and grab our banjo and work ourselves into a sound sleep. First thing on waking we laugh or skeer ourselves into another buck and wing, and so life goes.[13]

With this acute understanding of the ways in which commercialized depictions of blackness were being misconstrued as representative of African American life, Hurston was particularly troubled by the stage's perpetuation of minstrel stereotypes of blacks as carefree and impulsive dancers. Equally troubling, as her 1934 "Characteristics of Negro Expression" illustrates, was how quickly the profitability of black musicals had led white producers to take control of the form, leading not only to whites' domination of the theatrical stage but to the subsequent "whitening" of black vernacular dance forms. In this essay, Hurston launches a critique of white imitations of the black vernacular dances that she claims were born in the southern rural jooks, defined as "Negro pleasure houses": "When the Negroes who knew the Black Bottom in its cradle saw the Broadway version," she writes, "they asked each other, 'Is you learnt dat *new* Black Bottom yet?' Proof that it was not *their* dance" (62, 63). In declaring that

---

[13] A handwritten note on the manuscript indicates that this article was "killed" in 1934 for unspecified reasons.

"the dances [in *The Great Day*] have not been influenced by Harlem or Broadway," then, Hurston unequivocally seeks to differentiate her work from the popularization of black dance styles associated with Harlem night clubs and Broadway performances that played to mainstream white audiences ("Announcing *Great Day*").

And, in fact, when we take a closer look at the content and structure of *The Great Day*, the first of Hurston's revues, two things become clear: first, despite the claims of naturalness surrounding the concert, Hurston did indeed bring about significant revisions to the dances she had collected as she fashioned them for commercial presentation; and, second, the manner in which she transformed these folk forms helped alter the course of future stagings of black vernacular dance. Here we should keep in mind that whenever folk dance forms are presented in theatrical settings, transformations occur at multiple levels – from the duration of the dance, to the formation and facings of the performers, to the degree of improvisation present. Rather than focusing on the changes made to the individual dance forms, however, I want to foreground how Hurston offset these dance styles within her concert – how the conventions, frameworks, and performance styles she utilized influenced the meanings that accompanied the movement. When examined together, these nuances suggest the complexity with which an Afrocentric tradition of black vernacular dance was fashioned in the early 1930s.

Audience Reception and the Legacy of Minstrelsy

As mentioned earlier, Hurston's revues were set in a Florida work camp and recreated the daily activities of a southern black community. A surviving program for *The Great Day* reveals that the concert was divided into various sections; opening with a scene entitled "Waking the Camp," the narrative progressed from "Working on the Railroad," a series of work songs, to "Back in the Quarters," comprised of several children's games, to "Itinerant Preacher at the Quarters." After a brief intermission, the plot resumed with "In the 'Jook'" and then finally proceeded to the closing section, "In the Palm Woods," which contained the West Indian fire dance (*The Great Day*, Program). As the concert's content and setting demonstrate, Hurston attempted to solve the dilemma of how to stage vernacular forms without corrupting them by re-situating these forms firmly within a southern rural folk context. Presented on their own ground, the expressive idioms of the folk become a site for further exploration and appreciation rather than a point of departure to be extracted and elevated in the creation of a more "serious" art. In contrast to a typical dance number in a Broadway musical, furthermore, Hurston depicted dance as part of the everyday practices of a specific folk community – not as a free-standing spectacle, completely disconnected from the plot. And when we consider the physicality that each of these sections must have displayed – from the motions of the railroad workers as they lined the track, to the ritualized gestures of the children's games, to the social dances of the jook and the Caribbean dance finale – it becomes clear that *The Great Day* represented rhythmic movement as the driving force behind the daily activities of this southern black folk community.

The movement of the narrative implicit in the progression from scene to scene is likewise significant; this I will discuss in a moment. For now I want to call attention to what transpired between the various segments: according to the program, the well-known black actor Leigh Whipper, who also acted the part of the preacher, served as a sort of emcee, appearing on stage before and after each individual scene to help move the revue along.[14] Two separate reviews of the concert – one from the *New York Amsterdam News*, a black newspaper, the other from the *New York Times* – refer to Whipper's role as that of "interlocutor," although I want to stress that Hurston's program does not actually use this term.[15]

What is noteworthy about these reviewers' descriptions of Whipper as an interlocutor? The term alludes to a key figure in the nineteenth-century practice of blackface minstrelsy, in which whites blacked up on-stage and performed comedy routines, songs, and dances allegedly based on black culture, thus perpetuating damaging stereotypes about African Americans. According to historian Robert Toll, the interlocutor emerged as a fixture in the minstrel show during the 1850s, as a standard three-part format took hold. Characterized by his dignity and grandiloquence, the interlocutor typically sat at center-stage, where he played the high-minded straightman to the raucous comedy of the two endmen. Crucially, Toll describes the interlocutor as the "master of ceremony," an "onstage director" who facilitated the first part of the show to meet the audience's tastes (53). It is surely in this sense of a go-between or moderator that Leigh Whipper evoked the label "interlocutor."

But why did a revue staged in 1932 – eighty years after minstrelsy's heyday – elicit allusions to this figure? The fact that reviewers perceived Whipper's performance in terms of the minstrel show speaks to the continuing grip of minstrelsy on the imagination of American theatre-goers. Here Hurston's written

---

[14] While more work remains to be done on Leigh Whipper's connection to Hurston, research thus far establishes that he was a prominent African American actor on the early twentieth-century theatrical stage, later appearing in television and film as well. His successful acting career is mentioned in James Weldon Johnson's *Black Manhattan* and Tom Fletcher's *100 Years of the Negro in Show Business*, and he serves as an important source for the Stearns in *Jazz Dance*. Bernard Peterson's theatre directory reveals that he also helped Noble Sissle organize the Negro Actors' Guild of America in 1937 (145).

[15] See Illidge and "Rare Negro Songs Given."

references to the minstrel show's lasting impression on whites assume added significance. For although, as theatre scholar David Krasner demonstrates, early twentieth-century black theatre made serious attempts to subvert restrictive racial codes, there is no question that some believed, to quote Montgomery Gregory in a 1925 essay, that black musicals "fundamentally ... carr[ied]-on the old minstrel tradition" (156). As dance scholar Brenda Dixon Gottschild argues, moreover, "what has proven to be the most insidious level of minstrelization ... is the way in which that influence has persisted in nonminstrel cultural forms" (124). As if in illustration of this point, even the reviewer who one minute emphatically distinguishes Hurston's folk concert from other stage representations by insisting that *The Great Day* "offered something ... entirely *different* from that which we, in this part of the country, are familiar," in the next minute draws on the indelible imagery of minstrelsy to explain Whipper's role to her readers (Illidge 7, my emphasis). Regardless of Hurston's intentions, then, the appearance of a black male mediating figure in a revue of black vernacular music and dance indirectly but forcibly aligned her folk concert with a tradition of white expropriation and commodification of African American culture.

Strikingly, no figure even resembling an interlocutor appeared in any of Hurston's subsequent productions of this folk concert. Leigh Whipper did not perform in *From Sun to Sun*, which was presented in March of 1932 – just two months after *The Great Day* – and the surviving programs from all later performances of this revue indicate that the narrative moved from scene to scene without any kind of moderator. Although there is no way of knowing definitively why Hurston decided first to utilize and then to abandon this theatrical device, the fact that she withdrew the interlocutor figure provides valuable insight into her efforts to maintain control over the reception and interpretation of her concert by a largely white audience. A separate review of *The Great Day* that ran in the *New York Age*, another black newspaper, offers additional clues as to the function of this figure: tellingly, writer Lucien White describes Leigh Whipper's role not as that of an interlocutor but as a "master of ceremonies, introducing each group, with a brief explanation to the large audience of whites, with a few Negroes here and there, as to the peculiar meaning or significance of the presentation which followed" (7).[16] In White's portrayal, Whipper's part appears not as a vestige of the nineteenth-century minstrel show but as a strategic contrivance for navigating the knowledge gap between white urban audience members and the rural black folk depicted onstage; it seems entirely plausible that Hurston employed her "master of ceremonies" in just this capacity. Nonetheless, a portion of her audience insisted on construing the middle man as

---

[16] Interestingly, White's is the only review I have found thus far to critique *The Great Day* explicitly; he questions the authenticity of certain segments, faulting its depiction of the "exotic and erotic" as unrepresentative.

an interlocutor, and Hurston's complete abandonment of the figure suggests that she was unwilling to have her production read in the context of minstrelsy. Still, there is a larger point to be made here: with the presence and then absence of the interlocutor figure, Hurston effected an important shift in the position of black vernacular dance on the American theatrical stage. For while the *performance convention* of the interlocutor points to the vexed connection between African American vernacular dance and the legacy of minstrelsy, her *narrative structure* scripts an alternative history of diasporic origins – one that speaks to the culture of peoples of African descent in a broader, more global context.[17]

Narrative Movement and the Staging of Afrocentric Roots

As mentioned earlier, Hurston placed the West Indian fire dance at the end of her concert, which traced the daily activities of a Florida work camp from sunup to sundown. In other words, after immersing the audience in the folkways of southern black Americans, Hurston's narrative suddenly erupted into a display of a distinctly Caribbean dance form. In *Dust Tracks on a Road*, Hurston provides the following description of the finale:

> As soon as the curtain went up on the Fire Dancers, their costuming got a hand. It broke out time and again during the dancing and thundered as Caroline Rich and Strawn [two of the cast members] executed the last movement with the group as a background. It was good it was the last thing, for nothing could have followed it. (283–4)

As Hurston's comments indicate, the costumes worn in this section immediately signified the diasporic origins of the dance. A photograph taken by *Theatre Arts Monthly* reveals that the dancers were dressed in elaborately patterned attire; several also wore extravagant headpieces (Hill 19). The fire dance performers, moreover, were recognized by reviewers as "Negroes who had either just come from the Bahamas or were transplanted blacks who had kept alive, in surprising fashion, the forms and spirit of their native rites," thus further marking the Caribbean character of the dance (Ruhl 11).

Crucially, the style of the West Indian dance likewise differentiated it from the popular American vernacular dances with which a New York audience would be more familiar. As Hurston recounts, she was immediately struck by

---

[17] I am grateful for Kim Ellis' suggestion, made at the 1999 Black Theatre Network Conference, that Hurston possibly envisioned Leigh Whipper's role as that of a griot. The tension between these two interpretations – interlocutor and griot – is suggestive of the broader tension that exists between minstrelsy and diaspora. See Brenda Dixon Gottschild for a brilliant discussion of the relationship between Africanisms and the racist practice of minstrelsy.

the dance when she witnessed it while collecting material in the Bahama Islands. "It was so stirring and magnificent," she writes, "that I had to admit to myself that we had nothing in America to equal it" (1996: 281). Divided into three sections – the jumping dance, ring play, and crow dance – the fire dance involved a circle of players who took turns in the center performing various steps according to the rhythms of an accompanying drum. In a 1939 program for an exclusive production of the fire dance, Hurston describes the piece as "a folk dance that originated in Africa" and "was brought to Florida by immigrant Negro workers from the Bahama Islands," thus claiming an explicit Afrocentric line of descent for the form ("The Fire Dance," Program). The program explains three separate components of the dance: the first part, the jumping dance, required each performer to dance around a fire-heated drum of goat-hide until the drum grew cold; the ring play, described as "African rhythm with European borrowings," involved a single dancer who circled the inside of the ring seeking a partner as verses were being sung; and the crow dance entailed "a rhythmic imitation of a buzzard ... flying and seeking food." By situating this discernibly West Indian dance at the end of her narrative, Hurston created a scenario that gestured toward the roots of African American culture – thereby staging a theory of Afrocentricity long before the term entered popular or academic discourse. Moving from the United States to the Caribbean and invoking African origins through the ritualistic fire dance, Hurston's narrative effectively traced the Middle Passage in reverse; this Afrocentric narrative, I want to suggest, enabled Hurston to point towards the origins and evolution of black vernacular dance apart from the racist tradition of blackface minstrelsy.

In scripting this alternative history of roots, moreover, Hurston marked a turning point in theatrical presentations of African American vernacular dance, for her staging of West Indian dance within a narrative of diaspora soon became standard in the field of black concert dance, which, according to Susan Manning, took definite shape around 1940. The overt structure of Katherine Dunham's concerts throughout the 40s and 50s, for example, traced a forward progression from Africa to the Caribbean to the United States, thereby inverting Hurston's narrative order.[18] This straightforward, linear narrative of origins, furthermore, ultimately provided the model for many written accounts of African American dance history and is visible in such canonical texts as Emery's *Black Dance*, Marshall and Jean Stearns' *Jazz Dance*, and Jacqui Malone's *Steppin' on the Blues*. Hurston's alternative history of Afrocentric roots thus became the norm in scholarly chronicles of black dance in America. Yet even before these

---

[18] See, for example, the tripartite structure of Dunham's 1946 concert, *Bal Nègre*, Rpt. in VéVé Clark's and Margert Wilkerson's *Kaiso!* (98–100). Although I have found no definitive evidence to suggest that Dunham attended any of Hurston's productions, Hurston apparently rehearsed in Dunham's Chicago studio in 1934 (*Dust Tracks 285*).

histories were written, Hurston herself recognized the influence that her folk concerts had had on subsequent productions of black vernacular dance. In *Dust Tracks*, reflecting on the impact of *The Great Day*, she writes:

> I am satisfied that I proved my point.... Primitive Negro dancing has been given a tremendous impetus.... In that performance I introduced West Indian songs and dances and they have come to take an important place in America. I am not upset by the fact that others have made something out of the things I pointed out. Rather I am glad if I have called any beauty to the attention of those who can use it. (172–3)

While we can speculate as to Hurston's private feelings about the lack of credit she received for her contributions to this trend, her comments here verify that she understood the link between her revues and the turn toward diasporic roots in the developing field of black concert dance.

Geography and Choreography: Diasporic Transformations

In recent years, a number of scholars have submitted critiques of Afrocentric projects that posit a continuity between African and African American cultural forms. Paul Gilroy's *The Black Atlantic* in particular proposes that rather than perceiving identity as tied to "roots and rootedness," we should understand it "as a process of movement and mediation that is more appropriately approached via the homonym routes" (9).[19] Gilroy's problem with the concept of Afrocentricity stems from the way in which the assertion of cultural continuities seems to discount the memory of slavery; to the extent that Hurston's folk concerts emphasized the African roots of African American dance, they would likely be regarded as suspect by Gilroy. But a second look at her performances reveals that Hurston in fact anticipated Gilroy's theoretical concerns, for even as the narrative of *The Great Day* gestures toward the African origins of black vernacular dance, the choreography that operates within this narrative structure betrays a more complex and heterogeneous vision of diaspora.

Turning once again to Hurston's depiction of origins in *The Great Day*, then, the question that begs an answer is whether the concert's Afrocentric narrative suggested continuity or discontinuity between American and Caribbean folk forms. In other words, what was the nature of the relationship between North American, Caribbean, and African traditions that Hurston set out to portray? The scholar Hazel Carby argues that in her literature, at least, Hurston stressed

---

[19] See James Clifford's "Diasporas" and "Traveling Cultures" for further discussion of culture as movement rather than rootedness.

"a continuity of cultural beliefs and practices with beliefs and practices in the Caribbean" (40). But how exactly did the fire dance read in performance along- side other movement styles? To begin to flesh out an answer to these questions, it is instructive to examine briefly how Hurston treated such dance forms in her fiction, for just as Hurston's non-fiction casts light on her position vis-à-vis contemporaneous presentations of black dance, her first novel, *Jonah's Gourd Vine*, contains a telling portrayal of the fire dance. The dance appears in a scene in which a group of Alabama rural folks are gathered together with fiddles and banjoes around a fire. Hurston writes:

> So they danced. They called for the instrument that they had brought to America in their skins – the drum – and they played upon it. With their hands they played upon the little dance drums of Africa. The drums of kid-skin. With their feet they stomped it, and the voice of Kata-Kumba, the great drum, lifted itself within them and they heard it. The great drum that is made by priests and sits in majesty in the juju house. The drum with the man skin that is dressed with hu- man blood, that is beaten with a human shin-bone and speaks to gods as a man and to men as a God. Then they beat upon the drum and danced. (29)

The ceremonial performance lasts for several pages, until finally, "the shores of Africa receded," and the night comes to an end (31). In this case, it is clear that the fire dance figuratively transports the African American participants back to an African past. In Lynda Hill's analysis, "[t]he dance is rendered not simply as an evening's entertainment but as an occasion for the author to display her un- derstanding of African-American music's parallels with African performance traditions" (33). The fracture of the Middle Passage, furthermore, is healed through the performance of the dance, for, as Hurston goes on to entreat, "'I, who am borne away to become an orphan, carry my parents with me. For Rhythm is she not my mother and Drama is her man?'" (30). In this sense, there is little room for transformations among diaspora cultures, for black cultural forms like the fire dance provide a direct bridge back to an idyllic, pre-rupture moment; this is surely the kind of ahistorical invocation of roots which Gilroy finds problematic.

Yet in the very same passage, Hurston makes reference to the fusion of these diasporic cultural forms. In the course of the fire dance, as hands and feet clap and stomp improvised rhythms, Hurston writes, "Ibo tune corrupted with Nango. Congo gods talking in Alabama" (30). Her language here hints, as Hill maintains, "at transplanted African cultures *swirled together* in the nocturnal drama" (33, my emphasis). Although Hurston still claims the forms as African in character, they are portrayed as neither pure nor immutable, but rather as hybridized and "corrupted." In this textual example, then, cultural genealogies suggested in the enactment of the dance are ultimately left partial and provisory.

Returning to Hurston's theatrical productions with this knowledge, I propose that here, too, diaspora was presented as variegated and transformational. While there is no doubt that the narrative structure of these concerts traced a line of descent back toward Africa, or at least toward the Caribbean, it also implicitly showed how cultural forms shift and change as they travel across space. Recall that Hurston included a "jook" scene earlier in her concert, a site she considered important in the evolution and circulation of black dance forms. Presumably, this episode provided some illustration of social dancing that was closer in resemblance to popular American dance styles than to the Bahamian fire dance. We should also bear in mind the conventions of black dance with which a typical New York audience would be familiar – the shuffling, tap, and jazz styles that had evolved through minstrelsy, vaudeville, and black musical theatre. Hurston's concerts, therefore, were playing simultaneously with at least three distinct yet related dance styles: urban popular, rural folk, and (Afro-) Caribbean. What I want to suggest is that, in staging the *difference* between these conventions, Hurston's performance of diaspora subtly demonstrated the transmutations and discontinuities that occurred to dance forms of the African diaspora as they migrated from region to region. Remember, too, that Hurston herself described the middle part of the fire dance not as uniformly African but as "African rhythm with European borrowings" – already modified and hybrid in its Caribbean incarnation. For Hurston, then, Afrocentricity necessarily existed alongside revision and mediation.

Indeed, archival evidence suggests that in later productions of this folk concert, Hurston placed greater emphasis on the discontinuities between diasporic dance forms by inserting more popular American dances into her narrative framework. Surviving programs reveal that two of her 1934 performances – *All De Live Long Day* and *Singing Steel*, staged in Florida and Chicago respectively – contained sections devoted to "Buck and Wing Specialties" and to the "Shim Sham Shimmy," while retaining the Bahamian fire dance as a finale (*All De Live Long Day*, Program; *Singing Steel*, Program). As the Stearns explain, the Buck and Wing dance emerged in the late nineteenth century as "a combination of clogs and jigs and song and dance" (50); according to Dixon Gottschild, moreover, the term buck dancing generally refers to "an early style of full-footed, shuffling dance that was one of the forerunners of modern tap dancing and was a staple in African American minstrelsy" (121). The Shim Sham, meanwhile, was a standard routine involving a "slightly more complicated combination of tap and body movements," which became popular in show business around 1931 (Stearns 195–6). So whereas these two decidedly American dance forms had entered the mainstream via minstrelsy and musical theatre, the Bahamian fire dance had followed a very different migration pattern – one that developed away from the commercial space of the theatre. In juxtaposing these ubiquitous, recognizably black American dance styles with the imported, less familiar

Caribbean dance, then, Hurston invited her audiences to discern both the differences and the correlations between vernacular dances of the diaspora. In this way, Hurston's later concerts offered an increasingly complex and diversified picture of the Black Atlantic. Refusing any simplistic delineation of black vernacular dance, Hurston repeatedly modified the material in her folk concerts in a manner suggestive of the variable, transformational nature of the very dances that these concerts publicized.

Although Hurston's theatrical revues failed to generate any significant income, forcing her to rely on her writing for financial support, surviving evidence indicates that she nevertheless continued to stage versions of her folk concert as late as 1952.[20] As we continue to recover information about these stagings and the position of dance within them, we must remember to look below the surface of her own claims of authenticity. By looking at the strategic choices she made in transforming the vernacular material she had researched and collected into a discrete performance event on the commercial stage, we begin not only to apprehend the full complexity of Hurston's relationship to the folk but also to recognize the careful and precarious maneuvering upon which an Afrocentric concert dance tradition was built. In particular, close attention to the stage conventions, narrative structure, and performance styles that Hurston adopted reveals her concerts to be enactments of the tensions between the heterogeneous origins of black vernacular dance – tensions between minstrelsy and diaspora, roots and routes. *The Great Day* and its successors thus emerge as important landmarks in the ongoing contest to define the contours of black dance in the United States. Struggling to eschew a racist legacy that cast African Americans as "natural," unthinking dancers, Hurston effectively managed to re-script the history of black vernacular dance on the American stage even while she signaled new possibilities for its future.

Works Cited

All De Live Long Day. Program. 5 Jan. 1934. Recreation Hall, Rollins College, Winter Park. Dept. of College Archives and Special Collections, Rollins College, Winter Park. Rpt. in Hill, 24–27.

Allen, Zita. "What Is Black Dance?" *The Black Tradition in American Modern Dance.* Ed. Gerald Myers. Durham, NC: American Dance Festival, 1988. 22–23.

---

[20] See Hurston, "Letter to Jean Parker Waterbury," 6 Mar. 1952.

"Announcing *Great Day*." Beinecke Library, Collection of Rare Books and Manuscripts, Yale University. Program for *The Great Day*. Prentiss Taylor Papers. Archives of American Art, Smithsonian Institution.

Carby, Hazel. "The Politics of Fiction, Anthropology, and the Folk: Zora Neale Hurston." *History and Memory in African-American Culture*, Eds. Geneviève Fabre and Robert O'Meally. New York: Oxford UP, 1994. 28–44.

Christian, Barbara. "The Rise and Fall of the Proper Mulatta." *Black Women Novelists: The Development of a Tradition 1892–1976*. Ed. Barbara Christian. Westport, CT: Greenwood P, 1980. 35–61.

Clark, VéVé A., and Margaret B. Wilkerson. eds. *Kaiso!: Katherine Dunham: An Anthology of Writings*. Berkeley: U of California Institute for the Study of Social Change, 1978.

Clifford, James. "Diasporas." *Cultural Anthropology* 9. 3 (1994): 302–38.

—. "Traveling Cultures." *Cultural Studies*. Ed. Laurence Grossberg and Cary Nelson. London: Routledge, 1992. 96–116.

Creque-Harris, Leah. *The Representation of African Dance on the Concert Stage: From the Early Black Musicals to Pearl Primus*. UMI Dissertation Services, 1991.

Dixon Gottschild, Brenda. *Digging the Africanist Presence in American Performance: Dance and Other Contexts*. Westport, CT: Greenwood P, 1996.

Dixon-Stowell, Brenda. "Black Dance and Dancers and the White Public: A Prolegomenon to Problems of Definition." *The Black Tradition in American Modern Dance*. Ed. Gerald Myers. Durham, NC: American Dance Festival, 1988. 20–21.

duCille, Ann. *The Coupling Convention: Sex, Text, and Tradition in Black Women's Fiction*. New York: Oxford UP, 1993.

Emery, Lynn Fauley. *Black Dance From 1619 to Today*. 1972. Princeton: Princeton Book Company, 1988.

The Fire Dance. Program. George A. Smathers Library, Dept. of Special Collections, University of Florida. Rpt. in Hill, 60.

Fletcher, Tom. *100 Years of the Negro in Show Business*. 1954. New York: Da Capo P, 1984.

Gilroy, Paul. *The Black Atlantic: Modernity and Double Consciousness*. Cambridge: Harvard UP, 1993.

The Great Day. Program. 10 Jan. 1932. John Golden Theatre, New York. Prentiss Taylor Papers. Archives of American Art. Smithsonian Institu-tion, Washington, D.C. Rpt. in Hill, 17–18.

Gregory, Montgomery. "The Drama of Negro Life." *The New Negro*. 1925. Ed. Alain Locke. New York: Atheneum, 1992. 153–60.

Hayes, Frank L. "Campaigns Here for Negro Art in Natural State." *Chicago Daily News* 16 Nov. 1934. 27.

Hemenway, Robert. *Zora Neale Hurston: A Literary Biography*. Urbana: U of Illinois P, 1977.

Hill, Lynda Marion. *Social Rituals and the Verbal Art of Zora Neale Hurston*. Washington D.C.: Howard UP, 1996.

Huggins, Nathan. *Harlem Renaissance*. London: Oxford UP, 1971.

Hughes, Langston, and Zora Neale Hurston. *Mule Bone: A Comedy of Negro Life*. Eds. George Houston Bass and Henry Louis Gates, Jr. New York: HarperPerennial, 1991.

Hughes, Langston, and Milton Meltzer. *Black Magic: A Pictorial History of the African-American in the Performing Arts*. 1967. New York: Da Capo P, 1990.

Hurston, Zora Neale. "Characteristics of Negro Expression." *Negro: An Anthology*. Ed. Nancy Cunard. London: Wishart, 1934. Rpt. in *The Sanctified Church*. Berkeley: Turtle Island Foundation, 1981. 41–78.

—. *Dust Tracks on a Road*. 1942. New York: HarperPerennial, 1996.

—. *Folklore, Memoirs, and Other Writings*. Ed. Cheryl Wall. New York: Library of America, 1995.

—. *Jonah's Gourd Vine*. 1934. New York: Harper and Row, 1990.

—. "Letter to Langston Hughes." 12 Apr. 1928. James Weldon Johnson Collection. Beinecke Rare Book and Manuscript Library, Yale University.

—. "Letter to Charlotte Osgood Mason." 15 Oct. 1931. Alain Locke Papers. Manuscript Division, Moorland-Spingarn Research Center, Howard University.

—. "Letter to Jean Parker Waterbury." 6 Mar. 1952. George A. Smathers Library, Dept. of Special Collections, U of Florida.

—. *The Sanctified Church*. Berkeley: Turtle Island Foundation, 1981.

—. "Spirituals and Neo-Spirituals." *Negro: An Anthology*. Ed. Nancy Cunard. London: Wishart, 1934. Rpt. in *The Sanctified Church*. Berkeley: Turtle Island Foundation, 1981. 79–84.

—. "You Don't Know Us Negroes." Unpublished manuscript. Lawrence E. Spivak Papers. Manuscript Division, Library of Congress.

Illidge, Cora Gary. "'*The Great Day*' Heartily Received." Rev. of "*The Great Day*." *New York Amsterdam News* 13 Jan. 1932: 7.

Johnson, James Weldon. *Black Manhattan*. 1927. New York: Da Capo P, 1991.

Krasner, David. *Resistance, Parody, and Double Consciousness in African American Theatre, 1895–1910*. New York: St. Martin's P, 1997.

Locke, Alain. "Letter to Charlotte Osgood Mason." 18 Apr. 1933. Alain Locke Papers. Manuscript Division, Moorland-Spingarn Research Center, Howard University.

—. Ed. *The New Negro*. 1925. New York: Atheneum, 1992.

Long, Richard. *The Black Tradition in American Dance*. New York: Rizzoli, 1989.

Lowe, John. *Jump at the Sun: Zora Neale Hurston's Cosmic Comedy*. Urbana: U of Illinois P, 1994.

McKay, Claude. "Harlem Dancer." *Seven Arts* 2 (1917): 741.

Malone, Jacqui. *Steppin' on the Blues: The Visible Rhythms of African American Dance.* Urbana: U of Illinois P, 1996.

Manning, Susan. "Introduction." *Making an American Dance: Black, White, and Queer.* forthcoming, U of Minnesota P.

Myers, Gerald. ed. *The Black Tradition in American Modern Dance.* Durham, NC: American Dance Festival, 1988.

Moore, William. "The Development of Black Modern Dance in America." *The Black Tradition in American Modern Dance.* Ed. Gerald Myers. Durham, NC: American Dance Festival, 1988. 15–17.

Nash, Joe. "Pioneers in Negro Concert Dance: 1931 to 1937." *The Black Tradition in American Modern Dance.* Ed. Gerald Myers. Durham, NC: American Dance Festival, 1988. 11–14.

Perpener, John O., III. *The Seminal Years of Black Concert Dance.* UMI Dissertation Services, 1992.

Peterson, Bernard L, Jr., ed. *The African American Theatre Directory, 1816–1960.* Westport, CT: Greenwood P, 1997.

"Rare Negro Songs Given." *The New York Times* 11 Jan. 1932: 29.

Rosenberg, Rachel. "Looking for Zora's *Mule Bone*: The Battle for Artistic Authority in the Hurston-Hughes Collaboration." *Modernism/Modernity* 6.2 (1999): 79–105.

Ruhl, Arthur. "Second Nights." *New York Herald Tribune* 17 Jan. 1932: 11.

Sheffey, Ruthe T. "Zora Neale Hurston and Langston Hughes's *Mule Bone*: An Authentic Folk Comedy and the Compromised Tradition." *The Zora Neale Hurston Forum* 2 (1987): 49–60.

Sherrod, Elgie Gaynell. *The Dance Griots: An Examination of the Dance Pedagogy of Katherine Dunham and Black Pioneering Dancers in Chicago and New York City, from 1931–1946.* UMI Dissertation Services, 1998.

"Singing Steel." Program. Archives and Manuscripts, Chicago Historical Society.

Speisman, Barbara. "From 'Spears' to *The Great Day*: Zora Neale Hurston's Vision of A Real Negro Theater." *The Southern Quarterly* 36 (1998): 34–46.

Stearns, Marshall, and Jean. *Jazz Dance: The Story of American Vernacular Dance.* 1964. New York: Schirmer Books, 1968.

Stewart, Jeffrey C. *The Critical Temper of Alain Locke.* New York: Garland Publishing, 1983.

Toll, Robert. *Blacking Up: The Minstrel Show in Nineteenth-Century America.* New York: Oxford UP, 1974.

Toomer, Jean. *Cane.* 1923. New York: Liveright, 1975.

Walker, Alice. "Looking for Zora." *I Love Myself When I Am Laughing.* New York: The Feminist P, 1979. 297–313.

White, Lucien. "*The Great Day.*" Rev. of *The Great Day. New York Age* 16 Jan. 1932: 7.

Katherine Dunham's *Rites de Passage*: Censorship and Sexuality

Ramsay Burt

The censorship in Boston, Massachusetts, in January 1944 of part of Katherine Dunham's ballet *Rites de Passage* for being "outrageously objectionable" is only a small incident in the history of the Katherine Dunham Dance Company. Dance scholars at the end of the twentieth century recognize Dunham, who celebrated her 90th birthday in June 1999, as one of the major artists of the mid-century and dismiss the Boston censor's actions as an aberrant mistake. This paper proposes that the censor's actions and Dunham's response to it offer insights into an ongoing struggle between what I will argue was Dunham's radical, black modernist liberalism and a dominant white social and cultural conservatism. It is generally recognized that music and dancing have been among the most important means of black cultural expression in the United States, both as a site of dissidence and as a site through which to imagine and enact possibilities of liberatory alternatives to an unendurable present. By placing *Rites de Passage* in the context of Dunham's work as performer, choreographer and anthropologist, and locating the incident within its social and historical context, I aim to reveal the tensions between the expressive power of dance to make positive representations of gender, "race" and sexuality and the constraints placed on black cultural expression by dominant white society.

During the early 1930s Dunham studied sociology and anthropology at the University of Chicago and then, after doing postgraduate field work in the Caribbean, was involved in the writing and theatre sections of the Federal Works Project Administration in Chicago. As a result of these experiences Dunham developed, I believe, an extremely subtle understanding of the political nature of cultural expression. She knew exactly what she was doing in January 1953 when she refused to bow to American State Department pressure to remove *Southland*, her ballet about a recent lynching in the deep South, from the program her company performed in Paris. She similarly knew what was at stake when the Boston press mounted a campaign against her company's appearance at the city's Opera House in January 1944. It is this dance politics that I seek to uncover through an examination of this latter event. This paper proceeds as follows. First, it uses Paul Gilroy's idea of a Black Atlantic intellectual tradition to consider what sort of freedom Dunham imagined and embodied through her controversial work. It then discusses the ballet and examines the circumstances of its reception in Boston. While sexuality was the reason for its censorship, there are two other areas in which the ballet challenged white social and cultural conservatism: Dunham's position of cultural authority and her creolization of ballet and black dance traditions. Both of these were informed by Dunham's positivist, modernist view of acculturation and assimilation. My conclusion is that, when seen in relation to a Black Atlantic intellectual tradition, *Rites de Passage* embodies a modernist ideal of freedom and liberation.

In his book *The Black Atlantic*, Paul Gilroy calls for a concept of modernity that has "something to contribute to the analysis of how particular varieties of radicalism articulated through the revolts of enslaved people made selective use of ideologies of the western Age of Revolution and then flowed into social movements of anti-colonial and decidedly anti-capitalist type" (44). Gilroy argues that these Black Atlantic intellectuals:

> have contributed to the formation of a vernacular variety of unhappy conscious-
> ness which demands that we rethink the meanings of rationality, autonomy, re-
> flection, subjectivity, and power in the light of an extended meditation both on
> the conditions of the slaves and on the suggestion that racial terror is not merely
> compatible with occidental rationality but cheerfully complicit with it. (56)

He draws particular attention to a Black Atlantic reading of Hegel's notion of lordship and bondsman which is sometimes called the dialectic of master and slave. As Judith Butler points out:

> Perhaps because the chapter on lordship and bondage secured a liberationist nar-
> rative for various political visions, most readers have neglected to pay attention
> to the resolution of freedom into self-enslavement at the end of the chapter. (31)

For Hegel the bondsman attains the freedom that his master enjoys by choosing to submit to the master's view of reality. By internalizing a master, he develops a subject position through acceptance of the rule of law. Hegel's bondsman chooses subjection rather than death. Gilroy argues that African American intellectuals like Frederick Douglass who were born in slavery did not submit to the slave master's view of reality and actively preferred "the possibility of death to the continuing condition of inhumanity on which plantation slavery depends" (63). Dunham used modernist, scientific methodologies to analyze the form and function of what she called primitive dance. She also developed an unhappy consciousness which permitted her to recognize that the kind of censorship she suffered in Boston was not merely compatible with occidental rationality but cheerfully complicit with it. What I believe incidents like the one in Boston show, therefore, is that Dunham preferred confrontation to accommodation. Dunham, I suggest, understood liberation as a kind of Hegelian transcendence towards an ideal synthesis through acculturation and assimilation. She undoubt-edly saw artistic expression as the key site through which to claim the right to freedom and full membership within modern American society.

Dunham's education within the positivist sociology and anthropology of the Chicago School should make scholars attentive to the modernist, dialectical nature of her thinking about race. In the 1990s the extent to which both popular and some serious theatre dance styles in the West are creolized fusions of European and African derived dance and music traditions is increasingly recognized. Dance scholars like Brenda Dixon Gottschild advocate the use of post-structuralist and postmodern methodologies to theorize these fusions. If one looks at Dunham's work, it is clear that she herself understood acculturation and assimilation in modernist terms, thus subscribing to liberal, eighteenth century epistemologies which post-structuralist and postmodern theories problematize and undermine.

John O. Perpener, III, points out that Dunham must have studied the ideas of Robert E. Parks, founder of the Chicago School. Parks developed a theory which proposed that acculturation was a process that occurs in four stages. Initial competition between minority and majority ethnic groups leads to conflict, but conflict brings about a process of social self-consciousness which forms a basis for social and political development that makes possible the third stage: accommodation. The final stage, according to Parks, is assimilation as differences between the minority and majority groups are eroded. This account is clearly based on Hegelian dialectics in its view of assimilation as a resolution of conflicting antitheses. The problem with Park's theory is that the white majority have resisted accommodation with groups like African Americans and Asians whose inborn "racial traits" remain a visible source of racial discrimination. Perpener points out that Parks tried to move away from a biologically determinist model of racial difference by contending that different groups had characteristics which could contribute positively to the advancement of group interaction and assimilation. "For example, Jews were characteristically intellectual; Anglo-Saxons were restless explorers and adventurers; and Negroes found their most characteristic forms of expression in the arts" (25). My argument is that, if Dunham believed that the arts, and dance in particular, were means through which African Americans would become assimilated within modern American society, then *Rites de Passage* can be seen as a metaphor for this process of acculturation and assimilation.

Rites de Passage (see Illus. 3) was first performed as an illustration at the end of a lecture which Dunham gave at Yale University, "An Anthropological Approach to the Theatre," and received its premier in December 1941 at the Curran Theatre, San Francisco. It is thus an example of the way Dunham used her choreographic work to illustrate the academic conclusions of her anthropological research. It is a theatricalized recreation of imagined social rituals which, according to a program note, "do not concern any specific community nor any authentic series of rituals" (qtd. in Banes 151) but were intended to evoke something universal about the relationship between important individual life experiences and society's reaction to these. Her ballet has four parts: "Puberty," "Fertility," "Funeral," and "Women's Mysteries," although the last section was less often performed. Its title refers to the French ethnologist Arnold van Gennep's 1909 book *Les Rites de Passage* in which he argued that societies create rituals through which they mark the individual's or group's symbolic translation from one status to another. The process of translation, he proposes, has three stages: the initial separation, a transition or liminal stage, and incorporation. In a program note Dunham states that her ballet:

> can best be characterized as the set of rituals surrounding the transition of an individual or group of individuals from one life crisis to another. The ritual period, often at once both sacred and dangerous, is under the guidance of the elders of the community; the entire community joins in this critical transition so that the individual may, in a changed state, have a complete rejoining with the society. (qtd. in Banes 151)

I will return to Dunham's emphasis on the community's role in reincorporating the individual back into society later in this paper.

Tropical Revue was Dunham's first show under the management of the impresario Sol Hurok. It had its premier at the Martin Beck Theatre in New York in September 1943, where it was so successful that the engagement was extended until the middle of November. It was, therefore, still comparatively new when it reached Boston Opera House on 17 January 1944. Like her previous revue *"Tropics and 'Le Jazz Hot'"* it mixed pieces that were entertaining with some that were instructive in a variety show format. Some of these short pieces were based on dances from Latin American and Caribbean countries while others were based on African American dances from the plantation period. *Rites de Passage* was the longest item and constituted the centerpiece of the program.

This wasn't Dunham's first encounter with the Boston censor. In 1940 Dunham played the leading role of Sweet Georgia Brown in the Broadway production of *Cabin in the Sky*. When this went on tour, the Boston censor demanded changes to her costume. For one number Dunham danced with a bare midriff and a yellow diamond in her navel; this was necessary to draw attention to stomach movements which were part of her technique. But in Boston she had to glue the diamond onto a piece of paper so that her abdomen was covered. This was necessary.[1] The section of *Rites de Passage* which was censored, "Fertility," presents adolescents performing thrusting pelvic movements that ritualize sexual behavior. This seems to have been inspired by "Danses des Haunches" which Dunham learned in the Caribbean. In social dances like the Haitian "Congo Paillette," a whole crowd dances together with rhythmic movements in the pelvis which generate sexual tension. "If participated in at length

---

[1]   Katherine Dunham, telephone interview with Ramsay Burt: 21 Oct. 96.

and under the impetus of the crowd," Dunham writes, "this sexual dance reaches a climax and then releases this tension" (1978: 196). This passage comes from an essay on primitive dance by Dunham which was published in October 1941, a few months before the premier of *Rites de Passage*.[2]

"Fertility" shows village life, "with women pounding grain and men hunting and playing games" (qtd. in Buckle 53), and it is against this background that a man and woman are attracted to one another, their union then being celebrated by the whole community. During the central duet, the couple circle round one another rarely touching while repetitively performing thrusting pelvic movements which generate sexual tension both for the dancers and audience alike. This is also stimulated by Pacquita Anderson's insistently throbbing musical accompaniment based on a Haitian theme. The duet is carefully structured. Standing in profile to the audience, the young man and woman initially face one another, slowly clenching their buttocks and tilting their pelvises forward while their lower arms, parallel with their pelvis, push slowly forward and back. They stand back to back, the woman facing backstage, the man facing front, continuing the same movement, then return to face one another. When they have danced away from one another to each side of the stage and come back to meet, once more standing in profile center stage, the tempo of the music increases. This time the woman places her hands on the youth's shoulders while looking directly at the audience, while he looks at her and places his hands on her hips, rocking her pelvis from side to side in a horizontal figure-of-eight motion which is taken up by the other women on the stage, who each face a male partner without touching. As the tempo quickens again, the young man goes behind the woman once more cradling and rocking her hips with his hands as in a conga, swinging his head to the left as her pelvis rocks to the right, and vice versa. The five men behind them roll over onto their backs, each thrusting a flexed foot into the air, then roll back and circle, crouching round the central pair as the youth lifts the woman up in the air to the height of his shoulders. The music's intensity increases yet again as a chorus of female voices takes up its central theme and the youth pushes his partner upwards and she jumps forward to land firmly on the ground. The central couple walk up to a podium at the back of the stage for one more powerful lift. In front of them the other pairs of men and women lie down or crouch together in a final climactic moment as the music suddenly stops and the curtain drops. Dunham appears to have been trying to reproduce on stage the effects of repeating a narrow range of movements at length which she had experienced in Haiti in "Danses des Haunches."

One thing which Dunham was doing in "Fertility" was making a didactic point about the different ways in which sexuality is conceptualized within

---

[2]   There is a similar discussion in Dunham's subsequent book *Dances of Haiti* first published in 1947.

African and European communities. In his 1947 study *The Myth of the Negro Past*, Melville Herskovits of Northwestern University, who helped supervise Dunham's research in the Caribbean,[3] made some pointed observations about different sexual mores. "In Africa, and among those West Indian Negroes who are less sophisticated in terms of acquaintance with white behavior" (271), for a man and a woman to dance with their arms about each other is regarded as nothing short of immoral. "This reaction," he goes on:

> is exactly similar to that of Europeans who witness for the first time the manipulation of the muscles of hips and buttocks that are marks of good African dancing, or the simulation of motions of sexual intercourse also found in certain quasi-ritual African dances. Yet these latter are no more and no less lascivious to the Negroes than are ordinary "social dances" to white persons, where a man and woman dance touching each other. (271)

When one actually examines the central duet in "Fertility," the movement is not exclusively African in origin and involves not only touching but even, towards the end of the section, lifts. Dunham has, therefore, used African-inflected movement within what might otherwise be recognized as a supported pas de deux – the privileged choreographic moment of the nineteenth- and twentieth-century ballet tradition. Dunham's fusion of ballet and Caribbean and African American folk dance styles which contain African retentions received considerable criticism during the late 1930s and 40s. The leading critic John Martin, reviewing a company performance in 1940, complained about this:

> The group as a whole is handsome and competent, though there is among certain of the male dancers, including Talley Beatty, a distressing tendency to introduce the technique of the academic ballet. What is there in the human mind that is so eager to reduce the rare and genuine to the standard and foreign? (64)

Dunham and her African American dancers did not, however, want to be considered rare and genuine. They wanted to be accepted as standard and American.

Dunham decided to go on performing *Rites de Passage* at the Opera House in Boston. During the suppressed "Fertility" section the music and drumming continued while her dancers posed in a frozen tableau, thus falling back on a familiar defense of the lowly "flesh show": that it's only rude if it moves. The fact that the censors cut this scene doesn't necessarily mean that it was this

---

[3]   Herskovits is generally believed to have supervised Dunham's Ph.D. but this is not completely accurate. Having read through the correspondence between Dunham and Herskovits in the library at Northwestern University, Dorothea Fischer-Hornung concludes that Herskovits never agreed to be Dunham's supervisor. He wanted Dunham to move to Northwestern, while she wanted to remain living in Chicago so as to be able to go on working with her dance company. I am grateful to Dorothea Fischer-Hornung for this information.

particular ballet that had actually offended some Bostonians. Elliot Norton, writing in the *Boston Sunday Post* at the end of Dunham's week at the Opera House, argued that the Boston city censor was right to suppress part of *Tropical Review* because, he said, the performance was objectionable and outrageously offensive. He argued that Dunham's choreography clearly wasn't a "work of art" (a term Norton himself puts in quotation marks). Norton asserts the superior aesthetic judgment of Bostonians and hence his own right as a critic to exert cultural leadership when he pronounces that he, for one, rejects:

> the immature notion that any exotic performance of any kind which has been accepted in certain circles in New York is automatically "artistic" and ... the equally immature fear that failure to accept such a performance here [in Boston] is a sign of provincial backwardness. (n. pag.)

A number of celebrated censorship cases during the twentieth century have revolved around the question of whether or not a work is of such aesthetic value as to justify publication, or presentation. Within this view of censorship, the artist is often characterized as an avant-garde figure, somewhere on the Bohemian margins of society; from this standpoint she or he makes a highly valued, individualistic contribution to culture. Dunham as a highly educated African American woman could be seen to occupy just such a marginal position from which to make critical contributions of an artistic nature to white European and American society. For the white Bostonian elite, the question therefore appeared to be whether or not her work might be judged of aesthetic value; but underlying this was whether or not they were prepared to recognize the possibility of her making a valid contribution to contemporary culture and hence exerting cultural leadership.

Dunham, however, fits uneasily into the slot of marginal, individualistic Bohemian. Indeed, to consign her to such a position is to effectively ignore her African American identity. The black dance traditions within which Dunham situated her work were not the product of a small, educated, avant-garde coterie but of the non-verbal, and hence marginalized, African inheritance of a simultaneously feared (yet fascinating and desired) underclass of racial Others. Far from seeking a marginal, avant-garde position from which to speak, Dunham sought to identify herself with, and thus give cultural leadership to, the broad mass of African Americans. A sizable and sophisticated African American community had been living in Boston since the late eighteenth century. When the Boston city censor suppressed part of *Rites de Passage*, it gave critics like Elliot Norton the opportunity, in effect, to reassert their right to give cultural leadership not only to Boston's white inhabitants but to its black community as well.

The question of cultural leadership takes on an added significance when placed in its historical context. The early forties was a time of optimism for African Americans; 1940 marked the seventy-fifth anniversary of the ratification of the Thirteenth Amendment of the US Constitution abolishing slavery. In 1942 when the United States entered the war against Germany, Italy and Japan, many African Americans entered the armed services believing that fascism was a not-so-distant cousin of racism, and that with an Allied victory, "African American citizens would attain full citizenship and finally reap the benefits of living and working in a model democracy" (Powell 97). It is this aspiration that Elliot Norton in effect denied when he argued that Dunham's choreography clearly wasn't a work of art.

Margaret Lloyd, who wrote for the *Christian Science Monitor*, took a different view of the affair. Reviewing the opening night of *Tropical Review* at the Opera House in Boston before the city's censor acted, Lloyd observed that the performance "received applause that was not as large in volume as one might expect from such a large audience" (1944a: n. pag.). Lloyd disliked the revue's emphasis on show business and sex. The constant recurrence of sheer animality, she complained, was both boring and distasteful. Of *Rites de Passage* itself, however, Lloyd's critical judgment is perhaps surprising:

> When the prevailing theme [sex] is treated as part of the religious ceremonies of a primitive people, as in the male puberty rite and fertility rituals of the fairly dull concert piece, *Rites de Passage*, it has a certain dignity that demands respect. (1944a: n. pag.)

And Lloyd repeated this opinion in her 1949 book *The Borzoi Book of Modern Dance*: "The work was of a 'longueur' that was tiring, but of an integrity that commanded respect" (246). Lloyd placed the blame for the incident on Sol Hurok. Hurok's publicists were asking for trouble, she says, when they placed salacious advertisements in the local papers and sent out "lurid flyers quoting all the hottest remarks about the approaching heat-wave" (246). When the Dunham company returned to the Boston Opera House in December without *Rites de Passage*, they ensured that the show was taken more seriously. Lloyd, for example, was granted a long interview with Dunham which was serialized in the *Christian Science Monitor* (1944b). Dunham had, in fact, completely reworked *Tropical Review*. Hurok had a preference for light exotic numbers in a fast moving show. *Tropical Review* originally had eight short sections, but by the time it returned to Boston it was more Dunham than Hurok with three thematically programmatic sections: "Primitive and Latin Rhythms," "Creole Dances," and "Plantation Dances," and, as its centerpiece, Dunham's 1938 ballet *L'Ag Ya* replacing *Rites de Passage*.[4]

Dunham has a deep knowledge and understanding of the survivals and retentions of African dance and music traditions in Central and North American. Vévé Clark proposes that during the 1940s and 1950s a chasm separated

---

[4]   This is what VéVé Clark suggests in her essay on *L'Ag Ya* and *Tropical Revue* (Clark 1983).

Dunham's dance literacy from that of both her company and their audience. Although Clark doesn't directly comment on the actions of the Boston censor, in her essay on *Tropical Review* she implies that, if audiences had been more informed, the company would have had a very different reception in Boston. Clearly, however, social attitudes towards sexuality – and black female sexuality in particular – were a factor in the censorship of the performance. Clark points out that Dunham puzzled people by playing sexy roles when she was a serious anthropologist and was frequently criticized for it. Writing about the first night of *Tropical Review,* Lloyd was caught in this same contradiction when she complained that Dunham had a company of good dancers, but "her own dancing seems more willfully lewd because less unconstrained and natural than the others" (1974: 246). Class is probably a factor here: Lloyd, knowing that Dunham was a highly educated middle class woman, perhaps needed to believe that this sexy stage persona didn't come naturally.

American attitudes towards sexuality have, of course, changed substantially since the 1940s. Writing in the 1990s Sally Banes comments:

> That a beautiful black woman could be celebrated as a glamorous, sexually attractive person holding center stage, alluring precisely because of her vigor and power, and asserting control in sexual relationships, was a triumph for Dunham's generation, if not for ours. (156)

Banes is taking a liberal stance, assuming that it is possible to define a detached, value-free position from which to make aesthetic judgments with which all rational people (with a reasonable literacy in watching dance) will agree. This is the basis for her general position on representations of women in dance – that if one starts "neither with the idea that images of women are all negative nor that they are all positive, but rather, looks closely at the evidence of the works themselves, one actually finds a much more complex range of representations than has previously been suggested" (3). Probably both Lloyd and Banes would agree with this idea of looking closely at the work and at the dance movement itself. Nevertheless, the difference between Banes's celebratory view of Dunham's sexy stage persona and Lloyd's disapproving one alerts us to the fact that there are things which prejudice the kind of value-free movement analysis which Banes proposes. While it is, of course, necessary to base any discussion of *Rites de Passage* on an analysis of its movement content, we must also be alert to the prejudices which stopped some people in Boston in 1944 from looking as closely at the ballet as scholars like Banes have subsequently been able to do.

Dunham herself told Vévé Clark that during their wartime tours the Katherine Dunham Dance Company was "a floating island of negritude" carrying on a running battle against the color bar in hotels and segregated theatres across the breadth of the United States. We have seen how Dunham's floating island of negritude conflicted with conservative, white ideologies. *Rites de Passage* is probably the work within which the areas of contestation overlapped most potently. While it was not the only sexy piece on the program, it was, as Lloyd acknowledged, the most serious. Its censorship must, therefore, be seen not as an act protecting public morals but as an attempt to suppress the serious social points Dunham was making through the ballet. *Rites de Passage* drew on Dunham's sociological and anthropological knowledge to present what I have argued was an explicitly didactic representation of sexual mores. Its taboo blurring of racial boundaries through a fusion of ballet and black dance traditions asserted the right of her dancers to be considered not as exotic, primitive Others but as modern Americans who were part of a Black Atlantic culture. *Rites de Passage* is surely a metaphorical imagining of the rites of passage through which the black peoples of the Americas would finally be assimilated into modern society. No longer part of the African societies from which they had been taken into slavery, but not yet fully accepted as members of modern society, these disenfranchised and partly deracinated peoples were dangerous and marginal, existing in what van Gennep defined as a liminal state. Dunham's account of rites of passage, as I noted earlier, is less concerned with liminality than with the active role of the community in reabsorbing individuals into society. While on one level the ballet celebrated Africa and the artistry of diasporic African culture, on another level it imagined a future in which there would be a more universal, modernist transcendence.

Works Cited

Banes, Sally. *Dancing Women: Female Bodies on Stage.* London: Routledge, 1998.

Buckle, Richard. *Katherine Dunham: Her Dancers, Singers, Musicians.* London: Ballet Publications, 1948.

Butler, Judith. *The Psychic Life of Power: Theories in Subjection.* Stanford: Stanford U P, 1997.

Clark, VéVé. "Dunham's Tropical Revue." Spec. double issue of *Caribe* 7.1–2 (1983): 14–20.

—., and Margaret B. Wilkerson, eds. *Kaiso! Katherine Dunham: An Anthology of Writings.* Berkeley: U of California Institute for the Study of Social Change, 1978.

Dixon Gottschild, Brenda. *Digging the Africanist Presence in American Performance: Dance and Other Contexts.* Westport, CT: Greenwood P, 1996.

Dunham, Katherine. *Dances of Haiti.* 1947. Los Angeles: Center for Afro-American Studies, U of California, 1983.

—. "Form and Function in Primitive Dance." 1941. Rpt. in *Kaiso! Katherine Dunham: An Anthology of Writings.* Ed. VèVè A. Clark and Margaret B. Wilkerson. Berkeley: U of California Institute for the Study of Social Change, 1978. 192–6.

Gennep, Arnold van. *The Rites of Passage*. 1909. London: Routledge and Kegan Paul, 1960.

Gilroy, Paul. *The Black Atlantic: Modernity and Double Consciousness*. London: Verso, 1993.

Herskovits, Melville. *The Myth of the Negro Past*. 1941. Boston: Beacon P, 1958.

Lloyd, Margaret. *The Borzoi Book of Modern Dance*. 1949. New York: Dance Horizons, 1974.

—. "Katherine Dunham's 'Tropical Revue' – Primitive Dances Featured in New Show at Opera House." *The Christian Science Monitor*, 18 Jan. 1944a: n. pag.

—. "Rhythm Knows No Race." *The Christian Science Monitor* 30 Dec. 1944b: n. pag.

Martin, John. "The Dance: A Negro Art. Katherine Dunham's Notable Contribution – Programs of the Week and After." Rpt. in *Kaiso! Katherine Dunham: An Anthology of Writings*. Ed. VèVè A. Clark and Margaret B. Wilkerson. Berkeley: U of California Institute for the Study of Social Change, 1978. 63–5.

Norton, Elliot. "'Tropical Review' Called Offensive and Objectionable: Second Thoughts of a First-Nighter." *Boston Sunday Post* 23 Jan.1944. n. pag.

Perpener, John O., III. "African American Dance and Sociological Positivism." *Studies in Dance History* 5.1 (1994): 23–30.

Powell, Richard J. *Black Art and Culture in the 20th Century*. London: Thames and Hudson, 1997.

The Body Possessed:
Katherine Dunham Dance Technique in *Mambo*

Dorothea Fischer-Hornung

> I got a black cat bone
> I got a mojo tooth
> I got John the Conqueroo
> I'm gonna mess with you
>
> "Hoochie Coochie Blues"

Katherine Dunham – dancer, choreographer, instructor and anthropologist of note – had ambitions to be an actress. She had contributed as a dancer and choreographer in the films *Cabin in the Sky* (1943) and *Stormy Weather* (1943) and had successfully established the Katherine Dunham School of Dance in New York.[1] She left the United States to tour Europe in 1948. Her first engagement was planned as a three weeks' booking in London but stretched into three months. Over the next fifteen years the Katherine Dunham Dance Troupe toured over fifty countries as the largest non-subsidized, independent U.S. dance troupe of its day, with Dunham establishing more or less successful dance schools in Paris, Stockholm and Rome as well.

In 1953 Italian film producer Dino De Laurentiis was looking for a vehicle to showcase Silvana Mangano and to present her talent as a dancer, resulting in the Carlo Ponti-Dino De Laurentiis production *Mambo* (1954), a film which provides us with valuable footage of Katherine Dunham teaching Dunham technique and marks a significant step in clearly recognizing African American agency in cultural production.[2]

---

[1] Her success on the stage is reflected in the fact that box office receipts, not grants or subsidies, provided the seed money for founding the Dunham School of Dance in New York in 1945 and for sustaining it after it became the Katherine Dunham School of Cultural Arts, Inc. Within a few years over 300 students received instruction based on a holistic curriculum, emphasizing not only dance instruction, but also courses, for example, in languages, anthropology, sociology and psychology. Butterfly McQueen, Marlon Brando, James Dean, José Ferrar and Shelley Winters were among the students; José Limon, Lavinia Williams, Lee Strasberg and Margaret Mead were among the school's instructors (see Long 101).

[2] According to Roy Thomas, "Current opportunities for Black choreographers in Hollywood studios are directly related to the dance images reflective of the liberating and recreative powers of African-based dance and music. Taken together, *Carnival of Rhythm*, and the sequences from *Stormy Weather* and *Mambo* (1955) [sic] form the triptych of Dunham Tech-

Dunham had developed methods for teaching specific elements of dances she had studied and documented during her research in the Caribbean. She elaborates:

> Dunham technique is a series of movement patterns, isolations, progressions and exercises based on primitive rhythms in dance. These patterns create an awareness of time, space, form and function derived from their most basic inter-relationship. Dunham Technique is a series of exercises and movement forms, that if mastered, will flow in a logical order into combinations of movements and choreographic patterns. (qtd. in Rose 15)

The complex presentation of Dunham technique as portrayed in *Mambo* provides an opportunity to explore the racialized implications of the staging of a black woman dancer/choreographer teaching "primitive" dance[3] to a white European sex(ed) film star for a wide European and U.S. audience (see Illus. 6).

Mambo fundamentally challenges the tenet that the black racialized subject performs and dances "naturally" in that it visualizes rigorous formal dance training conducted by and for black dancers. In a 1938 interview conducted by Frederick L. Orme for *American Dancer* Dunham notes:

> [T]he Negro believes in a certain fallacy the white person has bequeathed him – namely, that the Negro is a *natural born* performer and needs no training ... *the one thing we face most often is a double standard of judgment, and the result is appraisal of good for the Negro that is far below the expected good of any other artist....* (59)

Dunham goes on to explain that dancing ability is not based on biology, but on rigorous training, even if this training occurs informally within the context of the activities of daily life:

> In America and the Islands we harbor an appreciation of this rhythm over and above melody. Of melody we have only a minimum, even in our blues and spirituals. But this appreciation is not based on any physical difference, nor is it psychological; we are sociologically conditioned by our constant contact with it, and it continues from babyhood up. In the West Indies, women dance to the drums almost until the hour the child is born – and they nurse it, still dancing. But that does not mean there is no technique. There is. And it is every bit as es-

---

nique in commercial films. Needless to say, the Hollywood films are not as rewarding for the student of dance as are those documentary films of Dunham choreography discussed earlier, but because of the far flung distribution of commercial films, this triptych has been seen by millions of viewers on both sides of the ocean" (113).

3   In Dunham's own words: "Perhaps it is relevant to point out here that the use of the word 'primitive' in connection with tribal culture carries with it no connotations of loose, inferior, or simple social organization. On the contrary, the West African empires which the slave traders invaded were highly integrated and formalized in terms of political and social organization and artistic development" (1957a, 4–5).

sential that we train as rigorously as any other group, even in presenting ordinary folk material." (60)

Yet, if *Mambo* challenges the assumption of "naturalness" in the ability to dance for black dancers, the scenes depicting Dunham technique being taught to a white dancer also suggest that the white subject can learn the techniques of primitive dance from a teacher who demands serious, hard work and dedication to a performance style with its roots in Africa and the African diaspora, a clear vision that Dunham had for African American dance from early on in her career. Her vision was:

> to establish a well-trained ballet group. To develop a technique that will be as important to the white man as to the Negro. To attain a status in the dance world that will give the Negro dance-student the courage really to study, and a reason to do so. And to take *our* dance out of the burlesque to make it a more dignified art. (61–62)

In a 1940 *New York Times* review, John Martin acknowledges the seriousness of Dunham's endeavor:

> With the arrival of Katherine Dunham on the scene, the prospects for the development of a substantial Negro dance and art begin to look decidedly bright.... Her performance last Sunday ... may very well become a historic occasion, for certainly never before in all the efforts of recent years to establish the Negro dance as a serious medium has there been so convincing and an authoritative approach. (qtd. in Aschenbrenner 34)

Other critics saw this in a decidedly different light, reflected, for example, in the titles of reviews of Dunham performances: "Torridity to Anthropology" (1941), "Cool Scientist and Sultry Performer" (1947), "Shocking Authenticity" (1963). As Aschenbrenner notes:

> These seemingly schizoid responses reflected an inability to reconcile elements that appeared to be opposites in their [the critics'] world view. Here, "primitive" was identified with "sensual" and "uninhibited" and was seen as the opposite of "civilized" (in the sense of "disciplined" and "cultured") and all it stood for. These critics could not reconcile the skill and discipline reflected in Dunham technique with their own stereotypes concerning the "primitive" or sensuality. The persistence of these dichotomies reflected the problem of critics in dealing with art which went beyond the limits of conventional modern dance. (53–54)

As scholar and performer, Dunham consciously intended to cross the borders of "low" and "high" culture, folk and commercial art, the "primitive" and the "civilized," the sensual and the cerebral, as well as the written and the embodied text. It is the complexity of "reading" the Dunham dance "text" that makes her work so challenging to analyze, for, according to Jane Desmond, dance, in comparison with oral and written texts, is "undertheorized" (2), and scholars have rarely "worked equally hard to develop an ability to analyze visual, rhythmic, or gestural forms" (50). Desmond elucidates:

> If we are to expand the humanities now to include "the body" as text, surely we should include in that new sense of textuality bodies in motion, of which dance represents one of the most highly codified, widespread, and intensely affective dimensions. And because so many of our most explosive and most tenacious categories of identity are mapped onto bodily difference, including race and gender, but expanding through a continual slippage of categories to include ethnicity and nationality and even sexuality as well, we should not ignore the ways in which dance signals and enacts social identities in all their continually changing configurations. (49)

This paper, as well as, of course, much of Dunham's own performance theory and practice, is intended as a contribution to the endeavor of exploring how dance in commercial film signals and enacts the complexity of socially gendered and racilized identities.

Capitalizing on the Mambo Craze

Mambo, a Paramount Picture release in 1954, was directed and scripted by Robert Rossen, better know for his *All the King's Men* (1949) and *The Hustler* (1962); it is generally, but perhaps unjustifiably, considered one of his weakest films. Rossen had left the United States after his testimony before the House Committee on Un-American Activities in 1953. His testimony on his membership in and later separation from the Communist Party and his "naming names" was the result of his own blacklisting in Hollywood, making it impossible for him to work and giving him time to do, in his own words, "two years of thinking" (qtd. in Casty 30). *Mambo*, acording to Allen Casty, was filmed, "to rebuild his [Rossen's] bank account after two years of inactivity" (17) and Rossen was presumably hoping to capitalize on the mambo craze of the 1950s:

> During the first half of the twentieth century, Cuba was used as a play-ground for U.S. business, diplomatic, and artistic communities. North American trends, fashions, and styles permeated Cuban radio, press, film industry, and literary circles. These currents brought changes in Cuban popular music and dance that were admired both domestically and abroad and were quickly integrated into North American movies, the record industry, and, later, television. North American promoters and producers ultimately diluted Cuban social and popular dance forms for commercial purposes. (Daniel 43)

Rossen later stated, "*Mambo* was to be for fun only," but he found he "just didn't believe it, got involved, took it seriously, and it didn't come off" (Casty

33). Here, his own evaluation underlines the serious nature of the *Mambo* project, and I would argue that more "came off" than perhaps Rossen himself and contemporary critics recognized.

Katherine Dunham was in a financial situation similar to Rossen's when the State Department refused to support her as a "cultural ambassador" on her European tours. And the financial strain involved in supporting a large troupe of dancers without subsidies might help to explain some of Dunham's more unfortunate adventures into film making, such as her choreography for the Abbott and Costello film *Pardon My Sarong* (1942).[4]

Mambo opens with a performance of a highly stylized, modernist mambo/boogie[5] performed by the Katherine Dunham troupe, with Silvana Mangano dancing the lead. In a 1957 lecture on Caribbean dance Dunham elucidates the urban, frenetic, anxiety-ridden context of the mambo dance craze which swept the urban centers of the Americas and Europe in the 1950s:

> The rhythm of the average metropolitan center is not one to induce integration
> – quite the contrary…. Our pace is uneven, our bearing has lost the composure
> of its stature and our spirit has no oneness with the air that we breath. We are
> dominated by a crosscurrent of rhythms and motions emanating from countless
> man-created machines and institutions, from fears, anxieties and loss of faith….
> A curious combination of jazz and bolero came out of Cuba toward the end of
> the 1940 decade in the form of the "Mambo" and has swept a tornado through
> the Caribbean, the Americas and Europe. Since the great waltz era which had its
> inception immediately preceding the industrial revolution, the social dancing of
> modern man, which after all is the sole vestige remaining to him of dance as a
> cultural trait apart from the theatre, has exhibited the increased neurasthenia, the

---

4   The cost of keeping and traveling with a major dance company was exorbitant. Dunham
    was also in the process of buying "Habitation Le Clerc" in Haiti, which she intended to turn
    into a culture and dance instruction center. In addition, the U.S. Internal Revenue Service
    was demanding back taxes. In a letter to Dale Wassermann Dunham wrote: "My tax situa-
    tion might conceivably prevent me from returning to America for a period of time" (see
    "Letters" of 18 and 25 Dec. 1953). The various Dunham schools, including the New York
    school, were never successful financially and Dunham invested a good deal of her own
    earnings in these ventures. In a letter of 31 December 1953, Wassermann suggests closing
    the school for financial reasons: "It strikes me that it [the Katherine Dunham School] is
    costing you somewhere around $800 monthly, money which could be far more useful in
    clearing obligations and establishing a healthier atmosphere." I would like to thank
    Katherine Drickamer and the staff of the Special Collections, Morris Library, Southern
    Illinois University, Carbondale, for their support in locating this and the subsequent archive
    material.

5   Desmond points out that Latin dances over time become "more and more codified and
    stylized and often pass into the category of 'sophisticated,' marked as sensual rather than
    sexual. The tango, rhumba, and samba all now fall into this category, as evidenced in their
    canonical inclusion in social dance classes and in national ballroom dance competitions"
    (41).

growing lack of integrative tendency and the fundamental disharmony in which we find ourselves today. (1957b: 4–5)

The Plot Thickens

The body of the film, with strong parallels to Mangano's own biography, consists of a flashback relating how Giovanna Mansetti (Silvana Mangano), a Venetian shop girl of lower-class background, became the star we see dance in the opening scene.[6] She is in love with Mario Rossi (Vittorio Gassman), a black-market operator and a part-time croupier at the Venice Casino. Giovanna meets the wealthy Count Enrico Marisoni (Michael Rennie) at the very moment that she is drawn by drumming to her first encounter with the Dunham dancers rehearsing in the Venetian hotel where she is waiting for Mario, who is looking for work as a croupier. Count Enrico's predatory character is immediately apparent in his comments on the drumming, asking if she likes the music. When she is at a loss for the right words, he completes her response of "Yes, it's so…" with a single word: "savage." This "primitive come-on" serves as a reflection both of his character as well as stereotypical assumptions about "primitive," i.e., "savage" music and dance. Count Enrico invites her to a lavish masked carnival ball in a Venetian palazzo. Giovanna, under the influence of a liberal dose of alcohol and the general license of the carnival setting, is carried away by the sexualized performance of the Dunham troupe, spontaneously joining them in an eroticized dance, complete with the lifted skirt and open legs, inviting *vacunao*, a ritualized, overtly sexual invitation in Latin dance.[7]

In 1941 Dunham categorized the functional aspect of various dances she had encountered in her research and also described the theatrical nature of Caribbean carnival culture, while speculating on their potential utilization and transformation if performed in a Broadway musical. She maintained that although its form would be altered, the function of these dances in social integration and as a sexual stimulus would remain:

---

[6]   The bleak portrayal of Giovanna's lower class background reflects Rossen's commitment to the Left and the tradition of Italian Neo-realism as well.

[7]   Yvonne Daniel describes this in her studies of the rumba in Cuba as follows:

Several other couples took turns looking for the possibilities of the pelvic thrust, or *vacunao*. I later learned that this word comes from the Spanish verb *vacunar*, meaning primarily "to vaccinate." Cubans coined it to signify this erotic pelvic gesture, the object of male pursuit and female flight that is the aim of the dance…. Some women came into the circle laughing, holding only one side of their skirts, almost daring the men to attempt a *vacunao*. When the accented gesture happened, the women adeptly covered themselves with their hands or skirts. (4–5)

> In these [Caribbean] societies the theater of the people ("theater" being practically synonymous with dance activity) served a well-integrated, well-defined function in the community; in the case of the carnival dances, of social integration and sexual stimulus and release.... What would be the connection between the carnival dance, whose function is sexual stimulus and release, and almost any similar situation in a Broadway musical – for example, the temptation scene on the River Nile in *Cabin in the Sky*? It would be the similarity in function, and through this similarity in function, the transference of certain elements of form would be legitimate. (qtd. in Clark and Wilkerson 56–57)

Beyond social cohesion and entertainment, Dunham notes the study of carnival "also illustrates that active psychological functions act directly upon the individual; the Mardi Gras acts as both a stimulus and release of energy, chiefly sexual. This release process might be called sexual catharsis" (1983: 44). In *Mambo*, Rossen and Dunham transferred this thesis to its logical European counterpart – the Venetian Carnival, where masked balls provide the ritualized context for sexual release.

Subsequent to this uninhibited, sexualized performance, Giovanna undergoes her *rite de passage*. Visually, Giovanna has no command over her personal space at the carnival; she is denied physical integrity as male hands reach out for her and touch her, aggressively invading her visual space, and literally grabbing for her after her dance. Enrico wrenches her from his male competitor's grasp, claiming her as his own. In the words of one contemporary reviewer, "the Count violently attempts to make love to her" (*Monthly Film Bulletin* 70) – clearly a 1950s euphemism for rape, indicated by the persistence of the Count's kisses, his rough hold on Giovanna, her futile resistance and the final sudden cut to Giovanna standing alone and depressed on an empty Venetian square. We hear her thoughts:

> It was daybreak before I could leave. Disgusted. Humiliated. I felt the need for revenge. I knew I didn't have the strength to do anything, not even throw myself in the canal.

When she subsequently meets Mario at the door of her flat, she confronts him with the truth that he had intentionally set her up with the Count, making of Mario not only the gambler but also the pimp.

While dancing in abandon at the carnival ball, Giovanna holds the attention not only of the Count but also of Toni Salerno (Shelley Winters),[8] who is cast as the manager of the Katherine Dunham Dance Troupe. Invited to join the troupe, Giovanna leaves cold, dark Venice for a sunnier future in Rome. She is

---

[8]　Shelley Winters had been a student at the Dunham school in New York and in 1953 was in a two-year marriage to Vittorio Gassman; Mangano and De Laurentiis were also married. The personal connections between De Laurentiis and Mangano, Winters and Gassman, as well as Winters and Dunham made of *Mambo* a kind of "family project."

driven hard by Toni, portrayed as a bitter and dissatisfied woman who had failed in her own career as a dancer.[9] Katherine Dunham plays herself, with her real-life role as manager, teacher, dancer, choreographer rolled into one, essentially divided between Dunham and Winters.

After discovering that the Count is a hemophiliac marked by death, Mario convinces Giovanna to marry the Count for his money, to which, it is implied, she agrees partly as revenge. But as fate would have it, Giovanna actually falls in love with the Count, who, unfortunately, dies after a jealous fistfight with Mario. Renouncing Mario and giving up her claim to the Count's fortune, Giovanna, in the closing scene of the film, returns to the Katherine Dunham troupe.

An "Artsy" Film

Generally, contemporary reviews of *Mambo* were negative; for example, the reviewer for the *Monthly Film Bulletin* describes the film as "pretentious and turgid," the "eccentric and unhappy" result of Italian and U.S. film cooperation, "another of these uneasy hybrid productions" (71). Yet, in the *Motion Picture Herald*, James D. Ivers focuses on the positive effect of the Katherine Dunham troupe "at their primitive best" (387) – a clearly positive evaluation of the term "primitive," yet laden with the attendant pitfalls of Eurocentric cultural bias.

Not only the melodramatic plot, but also the cinematography received poor reviews, the general consensus being that the dance scenes were considered simply "confusing" and "handled with no real flair or imagination," which could be read to mean that they were not handled like the usual Hollywood musical (*Monthly Film Bulletin* 71). *Newsweek*'s critic maintained that "the dancing of the Katherine Dunham troupe, which might have been enjoyable, is photographed so artily, however, that its charm is almost completely obscured" (49). Nevertheless, Jack Moffitt of the *Hollywood Reporter* did recognize the artistic

---

9   There are interesting parallels to Hitchcock's *Rebecca* (1940). In both films a poor girl marries into an upper-class, unaccepting family. The more striking parallel, though, is the implicit attraction of Toni to Giovanna, perhaps citing Mrs. Danver's adoration of the deceased Rebecca. Toni Salerno (note the androgynous name) may well desire Giovanna for more than just her dancing abilities: Toni throws Giovanna some very sultry, desiring looks; her lack of "distance" is visually represented in frequent, inappropriately close body space. Much like Mrs. Danvers, who fetishizes the dead Rebecca's living space and lingerie, Toni Salerno fetishizes Giovanna's dancing body. Danvers dies in the inferno of Manderly; Toni is killed off suddenly when she is hit by a car as she runs out of the studio after Giovanna refuses to leave with the company in order to remain with her lover, Mario. In both films, forbidden desire is punished with sudden, violent death.

merits of the dance rehearsal scenes: "Robert Rossen's direction seems most sure of itself in the drab slum scenes and in the exhausting rehearsal scenes of the dance troupe. Here he uses camera in a manner that, briefly, seems like genius"(3). It is Rossen's modernist refusal to stick to straight shots and his use of available light with special effects based on visual disruption through mirroring and montage with sudden, short cuts that rubbed against the Hollywood grain of the 1950s. These are the very scenes which I would argue are positive and interesting in their use of "hybrid" cinematography.

A Body Possessed – By the Mambo

It is these "exhausting rehearsal scenes," approximately five minutes of footage completing the first third of *Mambo*,[10] that take us from orderly instruction in Dunham technique, to Giovanna's collapse, to her eventual reintegration into ordered dance class sessions. Yet these scenes portray much more than dance instruction, and I would like to read the film as a whole, but this segment in particular, as an exploration and staging of "possession." A number of people in the film want to possess Giovanna: two men, one poor, one wealthy; Toni Salerno wants Giovanna as a star and perhaps also as a lover for herself; and, ultimately, Giovanna wants to possess herself and her talent as a dancer. But, I believe, there is another form of "possession" performed here – and that possession is based on Dunham's anthropology research on and initiation into Haitian Vaudun.[11]

The dance rehearsal segment opens with a view of Rome drenched in sun, marking the change of location from Venice to Rome. Giovanna's voice is heard from off camera:

> And so I left, no longer loving or hating anyone. Toni lifted me out of my unhappy life in Venice and took me to Rome with the troupe. I had dreamed of Rome – romantic and exciting, of gaiety and laughter. But I soon found that it meant nothing but hard work.

The first scene set in the famous hotel housing the Venetian casino opens with a close-up of Dunham in the right foreground in a second position lift with legs open, the palms of her hands extended outwards, a hybrid of classical and

---

[10]   The U.S. Paramount video release used for this paper is a total of 94 minutes long, of which the rehearsal scene is minutes 32–37.

   I would like to thank my colleague Michael Shiels for his invaluable insights into the cinematic interpretation of these scenes.

[11]   Vaudun is Dunham's own preferred Haitian Creole spelling, known as voodoo in the United States.

modern dance movement. In the left foreground another pair of dancers is only partially visible. In the background are two drummers. Dunham's upper body is lifted by her partner and turned out of the visual frame and returned when set back on the floor, spotlighting Dunham's significance as both dancer and instructor.

Toni Salerno enters with Giovanna from the rear, framed by the two pairs of dancers in the foreground. Dunham walks to meet them:

Toni to Dunham: Katherine, here she is. Make a dancer out of her.
Dunham [factually]: I'll try.

A dissolve takes us to Dunham in a dance studio, instructing racially and ethnically diverse members of her troupe in particular elements of Dunham technique. Dunham is heard explaining to the troupe that there are elements they need to work on because they "haven't been doing them very well," and she is shown demonstrating the movements in the background. A series of dancers is instructed at the barre, with Dunham teaching six specific elements of Dunham technique incorporating "body isolation": stretch and roll, second position plié, stretches ending with the head extended back, contractions with simple swings of the pelvis, and swing of the pelvis on twelve and back stretch.[12]

Dunham's knowledge of traditional Caribbean dance based on her anthropology research, according to Lavinia Williams, a dancer in the Dunham troupe, was a fundamental part of her instructional technique:

> Dunham's progressions were always creative as though she were preparing her choreography with the exercises. She stressed elevations. Basic modern dance progressions, such as walking, running, triplets, brush leap, all manner of leaps, jumps-sits or falls, and turns were also incorporated within her lessons.... Dunham used movements from ritual dances as exercises. She would break down the movements of such dances as *Yenvalou, Petro, Congo*, etc. from Haiti, or dances from Cuba, Brazil, Fiji Islands, Melanesia, Trinidad and Jamaica. (qtd. in Aschenbrenner 151, 154)

The use of available light, mirrors and dissolves in these scenes increases both visual depth and density. The effect created by mirroring, breaking as well as

---

[12] These scenes are documented in Dunham's application to the Italian Musicians' Union for the intellectual property rights to the scores of traditional music used in the dance instruction segments (see "Letters and Lyrics to Dottore Faccena," 5 Mar. 1954). This application documents the film footage shot, but also documents that not all segments were actually used in the final edited version. Especially the U.S. release was severely edited, making it a full 15 minutes shorter than the European version. The film has, according to the critic in the *Monthly Film Bulletin*, "undergone certain vicissitudes" in its frequent cutting and editing and it was "reportedly recut several times after Rossen finished it, and it is said to bear little resemblance to the original" (71).

multiplying the rows of rehearsing dancers, especially serves to destabilize the viewer's positionality (see Illust. 4). Like Giovanna, the viewer is at a loss for predictable orientation, denied a secure location and position. Seemingly insecure, Giovanna is additionally marked as an outsider visually, wearing a shirt and jeans, rather than leotards like the other members of the troupe. During the "simple swing" we hear Dunham's voice instruct Giovanna in the correct body movement and see Dunham's hands touching Giovanna's pelvis to guide her motion, and also forming her body during the head rolls, making of Dunham a creator forming the clay of Giovanna's body into art.

The film cuts to a different rehearsal room equipped with an upright piano. A Latin-looking guitarist and a piano player are positioned to the fore of the piano. A black male singer is to the piano's left with Dunham in the middle behind the piano. They are teaching Giovanna, standing to the right of the piano, how to sing. Dunham, who is clearly frustrated by Giovanna's lack of progress, asserts: "Now look, Giovanna. If you can talk you can sing," which, for our present purposes, could translate to, "If you can walk you can dance." Giovanna struggles with two lines of a song: "Black night, creep in; come hide my sin" and rebels in frustration: "I can't do it this way." Toni enters and admonishes her: "Make it your own. Your voice. Your personality," demanding that she go beyond imitation to actually "possess" the song and sing it in her own style. Visually, the "color-line" moves from the male singer, who has the darkest skin at the far left, to Dunham, who is more light-skinned and positioned in the middle, to Giovanna, who is white-skinned with long dark hair on the right, to Toni, entering on the extreme right, who is white-skinned with short blond hair.

The primal scene of Euro-American appropriation of African American culture has been staged. Yet, *Mambo*'s is a primal scene of appropriation with a difference: the Euro-American appropriation of African American performance style, which is usually invisible, hidden, is here explicitly visualized – a reverse minstrelsy scene: instead of "blacking up," we see diasporic African culture "whiting up."[13] In a 1957 lecture, Dunham pointed out that "the minstrel period of Negro dance" was particularly important in that "for the first time, the influence of Negro culture [became] apparent" (1957a: 16–17), yet she recognized the necessity of taking "*our* dance out of the burlesque to make it a more dignified art" (qtd. by Orme 62). In *Mambo* the whitening of black culture is explicitly staged as a black male singer and a black female dancer/choreographer commissioned by a white manager, instructing a white European dancer/singer, in the process transforming her from a talker into a singer, from

---

[13] See Dixon Gottschild (21–46).

a walker into a dancer.[14] *Mambo*'s performance of cultural appropriation never loses sight of the African diasporic cultural roots of Giovanna's art in its stubborn refusal to hide Dunham's (and the anonymous black singer's) role in this process.

In the third and final segment of instructional footage, we see Giovanna struggling with more advanced instructional technique. Giovanna has moved from the stationary barre to floor progressions. She is shown working very hard, driving herself, being driven, and she collapses. At one level, her collapse can be read as the result of acute fatigue, but I would like to suggest that at another level it can be read as something more subversive and interesting: as a staging of the "possession" of Giovanna by dance, more explicitly by Dunham dance technique.

The African/Caribbean singing and dancing style we see Giovanna and the Dunham troupe performing involves a good deal of twirling of the head and body, a technique used in many cultures to induce trance states.[15] Erika Bourguignon, in her cross-cultural analysis of the relationship of trance states and dance, notes:

---

[14] Dunham was not credited, for example, for her contribution to the choreography of *Cabin in the Sky;* Balanchine, a white Russian male immigrant, albeit a very famous one, received sole mention in the film credits. Dunham, writing in a "Letter to Goldie and Gumm," 17 May 1941, tried to negotiate the touchy territory of her intellectual property rights for her choreography at a time when Hollywood did not hesitate to deny them to African Americans:

> I am under the impression that Mr. Schubert saw the choreography, all of which was originated by me, for my concert performances at the Windsor Theatre, as well as that in *Cabin in the Sky* which was done by me ~~almost in its entirety~~ (changed to: "in great measure").

A note has been added, dated 18 May 1941:

> You will note that I did make one change, however, in reference to the choreography in *Cabin in the Sky.* It hardly seemed fair, in view of the fact that Mr. Balanchine cooperated so well with me to say "almost in its entirety," so that I have changed this to say "in great measure." I hope that won't change the body of the letter. (Special Collections, Morris Library, Southern Illinois U, Carbondale)

Her emphasis on Balanchine's cooperation with *her* and not the reverse is particularly interesting. Richard Long substantiates Dunham's view that she, and not primarily Balachine, originated the choreography for *Cabin in the Sky* (see Long 65).

[15] Ramsay Burt quotes Mary Wigman's description of her trance experience during *Monotony: Whirl Dance* (1928), derived from the Sufi whirling ritual, which reveals the dissociational potential of trance:

> Fixed to the same spot and spinning in the monotony of the whirling movement, one lost oneself gradually in it until the turns seemed to detach themselves from the body, and the world around it started to turn. Not turning oneself, but being turned, being the centre, being the quiet pole in the vortex of rotation.... And in that state only one wish: never be forced to get up again, to be allowed to lie there just like this, through all eternity. (180)

> Cult leaders conduct sessions in which mediums or potential mediums are taught how to enter into a dissociational state. This involves turning and whirling the candidate to induce disorientation, but he is not allowed to fall or lose consciousness. In the process the rhythms and dance steps characteristic of spirits are also learned, although these may not be taught specifically…. (40–41)

Culturally specific behavior must, according to Dunham, be adapted to enable understanding in a different cultural context, "My intention is not to reproduce an actuality but to get across the meaning behind the things seen and studied" (qtd. in Aschenbrenner 57). She stylizes in order to exhibit basic "truths," but is careful to retain musical themes and rhythms as well as to portray the psychology of the people she is depicting, incorporating the form and subject matter of a people's mythical beliefs:

> The conception of each dance is a thoroughly accurate one but the presentation is creative. I don't believe in transplanting purely authentic material to an urban stage in its original form, because I feel that primitive and folk material is functional in the community it's a part of. Its use in our theater should be purely derivative and creative. (qtd. in Aschenbrenner 57)

Mambo illustrates how Dunham uses spinning and twirling, head rolls, shoulder "shimmies" and thrusts, rather than specific dances from Vaudun to indicate trance-inducing behavior. Marking the passage of instruction time and also increasing the intensity of the experience as she had described it in *The Dances of Haiti*, with each cut the vocalization and drumming become more intense:

> It is the drummer of the *mama* who regulates the tone and pace of the dance, who decides when it is appropriate to introduce the breaks or feints which so often induce possession [in Vaudun], and who, by fixing attention upon and directing his drumming toward a particular individual, invokes the *mystère* [spirit] to enter the individual. (32)

In "Nan Guinin," the West African homeland, as in the diasporic culture of Cuban Santaria, Brazilian Condomblé and Haitian Vaudun, drums are essential in calling the loa, the gods which "mount" [16] a dancer during possession, in calling and communicating with the ancestors. Dunham describes her own acceptance as a North American based on the value Caribbean culture places on the spiritual and blood ties of the diaspora to West Africa:

---

[16] The title of Zora Neale Hurston's *Tell My Horse* (1938) refers to this process of the loas "mounting" initiates and is based on her own research in Haiti shortly after Dunham had left the island. The correspondence between Herskovits and Hurston reveals significant rivalry between Hurston and Dunham (See Hurston, "Letters to Melville Herskovits," 30 July 1936 and 6 Apr. 1937). I would like to thank Janet C. Olsen at the Deering Library, Northwestern University Archives, Evanston, who helped me locate this material in the Melville J. Herskovits files.

[T]he peasant priesthood acknowledges the blood relationship of all people whose ancestors hailed from Nan Guinin ("from far away Guinea"). When the stigma of being an American[17] had worn off, there was great and protective interest in the recognition of "Guinea" blood ties and great concern for my ancestors, who had not received the proper ritual attention because that group of slaves taken farther North had been cut off from their brothers in the Caribbean and had forgotten these practices. (1983: xxiv)

But as Lavinia Williams points out, the African musical principle of polyrhythms is also the basis of body isolation as a dance technique:

[I]n Haiti and in many countries, each and every part of the body is supposed to be dedicated to a god or goddess or even to nature. The feet are dedicated to the god of war, Ogun Feraille; the hips to the Congo spirits of beauty and love; the chest to the brave warriors, the Oguns; the spine to the snake god, the water god and the rainbow goddess, Pap Damballa, Maitre Agwé, and Mattress Aiyda Wédo respectively. (158–57)

This cultural codification would, of course, have been familiar to Dunham based on her many years of research in Haiti, as well as her *lave-tete* initiation into Haitian Vaudun.[18]

The title of the film, *Mambo*, can be seen, therefore, as a kind of play on words: on the one hand, the title overtly referring to the mambo dance craze of the 1950s, which, in the sexually repressive era, gave sexual expression and release in the culturally ritualized and accepted Euro-American context of ballroom dancing;[19] on the other hand, mambo can also be a covert reference to the term used to refer to a Vaudun priestess. The culturally stylized performance of dances such as the mambo in a ballroom setting allowed "middle- and upper-class whites to move in what are deemed slightly risqué ways, to perform, in a sense, a measure of 'blackness' without paying the social penalty of 'being' black" (Desmond 37); at the same time, the film makes Dunham the mambo

---

[17] Dunham's research on Haitian culture in 1935 took place immediately after the U.S. occupation of Haiti (1915-1934) had ended.

[18] A memorandum written in Venice dated 4 March 1954 concerning the carnival scene indicates that Dunham was very specific in staging her ideas in the film, including the final editing of the film. Her note, written late in the editing process, reveals strong commitment to shaping the final product, but also that she felt inadequately involved in the process.

[19] "In cases where a cultural form migrates from a subordinate to a dominant group, the meanings attached to that adoption (and remodeling) are generated within the parameters of the current historical relations between the two groups, and their constitution of each as 'other' and as different in particular ways. For example, the linkage in North American white culture of blacks with sexuality, sensuality, and an alternately celebrate or denigrated presumably 'natural' propensity for physical ability, expressivity, or bodily excess tinges the adoption of black dances. (Desmond 37)

who ritually initiates Giovanna into the knowledge of her spirit, sexuality, and ultimately her identity as a dancer.[20]

Giovanna's voice is heard off camera:

> Real dance was different from what I had thought: an easy way to make a living. I used to wonder if my strength to keep on came from my dreams of success or the habit of struggling hour after hour, day after day *for other people.* (my emphasis)

Giovanna, who is now dressed like the other dancers so she no longer stands out as an outsider, is engaged in a series of floor exercises, performing head rolls with diagonal leg thrusts and bends. The music becomes increasingly penetrating and the progressions more complex with vigorous dips of the arms and shoulders. As the dancing becomes more frenetic, close-up head shots of Giovanna increase. The camera is held steady from a constant frontal position, while seemingly uncontrolled bodies move in and out of the shot, with hauntingly spirit-like, even demonic movement. Dunham and the rows of practicing dancers behind her cross the studio floor from right to left and return from left to right. Mirrors on the back wall reflect the scene, dividing it into increasingly kaleidoscopic images with increased depth and motion of the dancing provided by reflection and refraction. The viewers' perceptions, paralleling Giovanna's loss of control over herself and her environment, are dislocated in space and disoriented, denied a solid, clearly defined subject position; with Giovanna, the viewers are literally lost and unable to know where they are, what is real and unreal, what is illusion and what is reality.

The drumming becomes more frenetic, and a male voice simultaneously shouting emphatically "Oomph! Ah!" is heard repeatedly, emphasizing as well as inciting the dancers' jutting, vigorous movements.[21] A high female singing

---

[20] Bourguignon elaborates on the culturally stylized performativity of trance dance and the identities portrayed:

> What, then, is the relationship between the dance on the one hand and states of altered consciousness, be they trance or possession trance, on the other? Dance, as we have indicated, appears to have two principal points of contract with such states. In the visionary trances the former appears to be primarily the case, while in states of possession trance both appear to be equally relevant and important. In particular, the behavior of the spirit who is supposed to possess the trancer may involve characteristic choreographic features.... [T]rances are above all culturally stylized performances and experiences. (Bourguignon 56–7)

[21] Lavinia Williams describes this particular element of the Dunham technique:

> There is one exercise throughout that is like a Dunham trademark. It was done in *Rites de Passage*, and I have never seen a teacher of Dunham technique who does not do this movement.... This movement begins in wide second, demi-plié; jumps in this position, sometimes doing bell kicks, open leg leaps, etc.

voice intrudes as the drumming and twirling of the dancers reach a fevered pitch. Visual and auditory energy increases, as do the head rolls and the demon-like thrusting and jumping of dancing bodies across the screen. Giovanna collapses with the camera focused on an extremely ambiguous close up of her facial expression. Is what we see exhaustion? Ecstasy? Trance? Dunham and an anonymous white male dancer, who has been consistently positioned next to or very near Giovanna throughout the rehearsals, rush in to help her, lifting her off the floor (see Illus. 5). They guide her to a couch in the next room, a separate, calm and controlled space dominated by Toni:

Toni to Dunham:	I'll take care of her. [hands Giovanna a glass of water]
Toni to Giovanna	You feel better? Get back to work [begins to pull her off the couch].
Giovanna:	I can't. I'm not a machine.
Toni:	That's exactly what you are. Until you're a dancer, you're a machine. Come on.

Giovanna returns to the rehearsal and participates in the floor progressions, which are now once again performed in controlled lines of dancers; order has been reestablished.

Nevertheless, the representation of Mangiano's "possession" raises several interesting questions about the racial politics of *Mambo*. Silvana Mangano, the white Italian female sexualized body, is visualized working in the context of a racially and sexually mixed company of dancers. At the barre she is initially positioned between a black male dancer in the foreground and the anonymous white dancer, who, like Giovanna, is not in warm-up clothes and appears to be uncertain and new to the group. She is consistently shown next to him in the formations during the floor exercises. While physical activity and twirling motion generally become more frenetic and driven, he visually initiates the trance/possession scene. We see him throwing up his arm to his face and almost stumbling, looking confused or frightened, surrounded by the movement of the other "possessed/tranced" dancers. He stumbles slightly, seems to lose his balance and flees to the right foreground and then stumbles off camera. When Giovanna collapses, he reenters, and it is this white male dancer that initially picks her up from the floor and carries her into the next room.

A favorite variation, and one used in *Rites de Passage* was a jump in second once, jump and cross the leg right in front of the left, left arm contracted towards the right leg (right leg is in fourth position front, bent), jump again in second and then jump across. The same exercise was repeated in half turns and jumps, then full turns without stopping, and ending with jumps in second position. (qtd. in Aschenbrenner 150)

In the context of the 1950s, these racially integrated and erotically charged dance scenes are certainly quite unusual, and it is presumably the European context that made this possible.[22] Yet it is certainly not accidental that Giovanna's out-of-control, collapsed body is picked up and carried by the white male dancer rather than any of her darker skinned co-dancers – there are, assuredly, limits to how radically a European film in the 1950s could cross the racial borders of desire. It is only after he has lifted her up that Dunham runs in to help him carry her to a couch. Just as in the carnival scenes, men consistently invade Giovanna's physical integrity. Although it is portrayed as a gentle, caring gesture, the male dancer takes the liberty of quickly stroking her face at the very moment Giovanna does not have control over her body. White male hegemony has been effectively reestablished until Giovanna "comes to" and reestablishes control over her white sexualized body. Again, as in the primal scene of the appropriation of African American song culture, it is Toni Salerno, the white female manager, who "re-possesses" Giovanna and sends her back to work with Dunham and her troupe.

Only after Giovanna is willing to give herself up to the discipline of her muse can she move beyond being passively possessed by dance and actively begin to possess the dance herself – a distinction that is certainly not foreign to the culture of trance and possession:

> The event [possession] is not a matter of domination, but a kind of *double movement of attenuation and expansion*.... And the possessed gives herself up to become an instrument in a social and communicative drama. This experience of election, its shock of communion, is not evidence of psychic disruption, or proof of pathology, but rather a result of the *most intense discipline and study*. Not everyone can be possessed, for not everyone can know how to respond to the demands and expectations of her god. (Dayan 40; my emphasis)

Toni is absolutely accurate in her assertion that until Giovanna has appropriated the Dunham technique, until she has, so to speak, "paid her dues" to the hard task master, the mambo, and makes it her own, she is a machine – without

---

22 According to Dunham, "Without Europe we couldn't have survived" (qtd. in Aschenbrenner 35). She had sufficient experience with segregation in the U.S.A., where often her troupe was not allowed to stay in the same venues where she performed. Dunham's statement after her 19 Oct. 1944 performance in Louisville, Kentucky, asserting her unwillingness to perform again in the city until racism was eliminated, caused a major stir. (See Clark and Wilkerson 85–88).

But Europe was not without its own form of racial politics. In a 1948 article in the *The London Observer*, the racialized politics of Dunham's performances are addressed and the critic, although presumably trying to set himself off from those who felt racial integration was a problem, feels moved to comment on her "white husband, John Pratt," and on the fact that "her school is racially 'mixed,' and, therefore, controversial amongst the 'whites' ..." (qtd. in Clark and Wilkerson 107).

soul or vitality. Although she has not made it her own yet, *dance* has been in the process of making her *its* own.[23]

The final scene of the film, after Giovanna has loved and lost the Count as well as separated from Mario, once again visualizes the hybridity that was so disturbing to contemporary critics. She walks into the theater where in a long shot from the back of the theater over the theater's empty seats, she, as well as the film viewer through the "eye" of the camera behind her, watches the Katherine Dunham troupe performing classical ballet exercises on the stage. Giovanna's thoughts are verbalized in the voice over:

> And now I was leaving Enrico's world – a world I had entered wearing a mask at a carnival ball – and I was leaving Mario's world, the world into which I had been born. There was left only what I had learned through work – that and my talent as dancer. Perhaps in my third world, the absorbing world of the Mambo, I could find forgetfulness of the past – in time peace and happiness.

Though the dance warm-ups we see staged in the closing sequence are quite classical, the sound track disrupts the desire for a harmonious resolution. We hear not *Swan Lake* or the *Nutcracker Suite*, but rather the theme music composed by Bernardo Noriega,[24] a very modern, jazzy, African-Latin-European hybrid mambo. And just like the mambo, which is an urban Afro-European dance form, Dunham's choreography, with its liberating, African-Caribbean-European creolized dance style, has the potential to liberate Giovanna in her expression of herself in "otherness." As Ramsay Burt points out:

> To dance is to take into and find within one's own body possibilities of moving that expresses otherness.... to dance in this way is to reject ideologies of national and "racial" identity (and superiority), and to thus blur boundaries that have been defined as tight and rigid. (195)

---

[23] The is the theme of a dancer who has to give up everything to possess her talent as a dancer under the tutelage of an extremely demanding instructor had, of course, been explored several years earlier in the film *The Red Shoes* (1948, directed by Michael Powell and Emeric Pressburger), based on the fairy tale written by Hans Christian Anderson. I would like to thank Susan Jones of Oxford University who pointed out the similarity in theme during a discussion of this paper at National University of Ireland, Galway, in September 2000.

[24] Some of the music and many of the lyrics were provided by Katherine Dunham, and there is correspondence to indicate that she had difficulties in registering her copyright with the Italian musicians' union. This became particularly important after she learned that two of the songs, for example, the blues Mangiano sings in the last third of the film, had been re-corded for record production. Considering the popularity of Mangano, this was surely a serious financial consideration (See Dunham "Letters, Lyrics and Lists of Titles of Music" 11 and 12 Nov. 1954).

In order to attain her identity, Giovanna must remove the imposed cultural mask imposed by her class, sex and racial origin, as well as the demands of all those who want to possess her from outside herself.

We see Giovanna look over her shoulder at us, at the unseen viewer; she nods slightly, as if to acknowledge us and to receive the approval of those who know the story of her past. She turns and walks away from us onto the stage and into her future. The white girl and the black girl, it is implied, *can* dance in the space provided by a culture open enough to embrace their hybridity. In the voiceover, Dunham, in an invitation to possess this hybridity, to change her "skin," has the last word: "Go change your clothes."

Conclusion

Ultimately, the question remains: If this film was intended to be a part of Dunham's project to liberate modernist dance from the strictures of racialized ideology that attributes physical "naturalness" to the African American body and dance, does the film actually succeed in conveying this message?

The intended logic of *Mambo* would, presumably, indicate that after thorough training in Dunham technique, Giovanna would be such an accomplished dancer that she would become a star and could hold her own with the Dunham troupe. Unfortunately, Mangano's talent as a dancer revealed in the opening mambo/boogie is not sufficient to support this interpretation – she simply never dances up to the standards of the Dunham troupe. In a reaction that is typical, John Moffitt in the *Hollywood Reporter* comments:

> [T]he footage required to fake her terpsichorean talents keeps the audience from seeing much of the Katherine Dunham troupe of Negro dancers who can perform superlatively well. This gives the film a certain aggravating quality to sophisticated audiences. When you know that the justly famous Miss Dunham and her company are present, you naturally want to see them really cut loose. It also confuses the story, since it is hard to see why an organization that has so specialized in Negro choreography and music as to place it among the top modern arts should want to spend so much trouble featuring a white performance. (3)

Granted, value-free aesthetic judgment of the racialized body was certainly impossible in the 1950s, as it still is, which is clearly reflected in the comments on the "sophisticated audience's" wish to see "Negro choreography and music" really "cut loose." It would have required a dancer of extraordinary ability, which Mangano is not, to transcend such stereotypical assumptions. Desmond asks: "What happens when people who are already marginalized as being *only* their bodies enter an art form that is similarly positioned as physical, intuitive, emotional, and nonintellectual?" (7). She maintains that even when a legitimate attempt is made to cut through traditional racialized body concepts, "the representational structures of traditional gazes are not really challenged … [causing] performances like these [to] easily slip back into a racist ideology that frames the dancers as spectacles of the 'other,' as black bodies that are inherently exuberant and naturally rhythmic" (Desmond 25) or, in analogy, white bodies that are inherently cold and naturally cerebral. In *Mambo* the racialized white body in its appropriation of black dance forms fails to transcend this essentialism. What, unfortunately, the audience ultimately does see, I believe, is: "White girls can't dance," undermining Dunham's project to liberate the black dancing body from racialized "primitivism" and the white body from equally racialized "culturalism." We are caught in an essentialist trap.

It is clearly in the context of her individual dream that Giovanna looks for fulfillment in dance, but it is in the community of dancers that she must learn to try to fulfill this dream. It is the individual body that is the medium, but it is the community of music and dance that expresses this in Rossen's film. If *Mambo* started out as a showcase for Silvana Mangiano as a dancer, it has given us, in the end, an invaluable documentation not only of the Dunham technique but also an indication of what it might mean for a dancer to transcend the racialized body.

In the context of a European "art film," *Mambo* provides a unique multivalent documentation of Katherine Dunham teaching her technique, as well as her attempt to implement intercultural understanding based on specifically grounded African diasporic cultural forms. Dance is documented as a learned discipline, enabling the dancer to be possessed by and to possess the liberation of body and spirit in dance. *Mambo* marks a brave attempt to transcend the boundaries of the culturally racialized dancing body, a film that takes itself and, more significantly, Dunham's contribution to modern dance culture seriously.

Works Cited

Albright, Ann Cooper. *Choreographing Difference: The Body and Identity in Contemporary Dance.* Hanover: Wesleyan UP, 1997.

Aschenbrenner, Joyce. ed. *Katherine Dunham: Reflections on the Social and Political Contexts of Afro-American Dance.* Dance Research Annual XII. New York: CORD, 1981.

Bourguignon, Erika. "Trance Dance." *Dance Perspectives* 34 (1968): 1–61.

Burt, Ramsay. *Alien Bodies: Representations of Modernity, 'Race' and Nation in Early Modern Dance.* London: Routledge, 1998.

Casty, Alan. *The Films of Robert Rossen*. New York: Museum of Modern Art, 1969.

Clark, VèVè A., and Margaret B. Wilkerson. eds. *Kaiso! Katherine Dunham: An Anthology of Writings*. Berkeley: U of California Institute for the Study of Social Change, 1978.

Daniel, Yvonne. *Rumba: Dance and Social Change in Contemporary Cuba*. Bloomington: Indiana UP, 1995.

Dayan, Joan. "Vodoun, or the Voices of the Gods. " *Raritan* 10.3 (1991): 32–57.

Desmond, Jane C. *Meaning in Motion: New Cultural Studies in Dance*. Durham: Duke UP, 1997.

Dixon Gottschild, Brenda. *Digging the Africanist Presence in American Performance: Dance and Other Contexts*. Westport, CT: Greenwood, 1996.

Dunham, Katherine. *The Dances of Haiti*. Rev. ed. Los Angeles: Center for Afro-American Studies, U of California, 1983.

—. "Letters to Dale Wasserman." 18 and 25 December 1953. Special Collections. Morris Library, Southern Illinois U, Carbondale.

—. "Letter to Dott. Enrico Lonardi." 12 Nov. 1954 (3 pages). Special Collections. Morris Library, Southern Illinois U, Carbondale.

—. "Letter and Song Lyrics to Dottore Faccena." 5 Mar. 1954 (8 pages). Special Collections. Morris Library, Southern Illinois U, Carbondale.

—. "Letters, Lyrics and Lists of Titles of Music submitted to Societa Iatliana [sic] degli Autori ed Editori." 11 Nov. 1954 (2 pages). Special Collections. Morris Library, Southern Illinois U, Carbondale.

—. Letters, Lyrics and Lists of Titles of Music to Datt. Enrico Lonardi." 12 Nov. 1954 (12 pages). Special Collections. Morris Library, Southern Illinois U, Carbondale.

—. "Letter to Goldie and Gumm." 17 May 1941 with correction dated 18 May 1941. Special Collections. Morris Library, Southern Illinois U, Carbondale.

—. "Memorandum to Robert Rossen." 4 March 1954. Special Collections. Morris Library, Southern Illinois U, Carbondale.

—. "The Role of Dance in Primitive Society (With Special Emphasis on the West Indies)." Lecture, n.d. [Mar. 1957?a], 1–20. Special Collections, Morris Library, Southern Illinois U, Carbondale.

—. "The Role of Dance in Primitive Society (With Special Emphasis on the West Indies)." Lecture, Mar. 1957b, 1–9. Special Collections. Morris Library, Southern Illinois U, Carbondale.

—. "Titles as Recorded" [carbon copy]. 19 Nov. 1954 (1 page). Special Collections. Morris Library, Southern Illinois U, Carbondale.

—. "Thesis Turned Broadway." *California Arts and Architecture*. 1941. Rpt. in *Kaiso! Katherine Dunham: An Anthology of Writings*. Ed. VèVè A. Clark and

Margaret B. Wilkerson. Berkeley: U of California Institute for the Study of Social Change, 1978. 56–57.

Hurston, Zora Neale. "Letters to Melville Herskovits." 6 Apr. 1937 and 30 July 1936. The Melville J. Herskovits Files. Deering Library, Northwestern U Archives, Evanston.

—. *Tell My Horse: Voodoo and Life in Haiti and Jamaica.* 1938. New York: Harper and Row, 1990.

Ivers, James D. "*Mambo* – Tangled Web." Rev. *Motion Picture Herald* 2 April 1955: 387.

"Katherine Dunham." *London Observer,* 12. Sept. 1948. Rpt. in *Kaiso! Katherine Dunham: An Anthology of Writings.* Ed. VèVè A. Clark and Margaret B. Wilkerson. Berkeley: U of California Institute for the Study of Social Change, 1978. 107.

Long, Richard. *The Black Tradition in American Dance.* London: Prion, 1989.

Mambo. Dir. Robert Rossen. Prod. Carlo Ponti, Dino De Laurentiis. Screen Play by Guido Piovene, Ivo Perilli, Ennio de Concini, Robert Rossen. Perf. Silvana Mangano, Michael Rennie, Vittorio Gassman, Shelly Winters and Katherine Dunham. Paramount Pictures, 1954. B&W, 94 minuites. VHS Dist. Hen's Tooth Video, 1991.

Moffitt, Jack. "*Mambo* Drab Foreign Yarn: Italian-Made Film Is Too Depressing." Rev. of *Mambo. Hollywood Reporter* 29 Mar. 1955: 3.

Monthly Film Bulletin. Rev. of *Mambo.* Jan. 1955: 70–71.

Newsweek. Rev. of *Mambo.* 18 Apr. 1955: 3.

Noriega, Bernardo. "Letters to Societa Iatliana [sic] degli Autori ed Editori." 11 Nov. 1954 (1 page Italian; 1 page English). Special Collections. Morris Library, Southern Illinois U, Carbondale.

Orme, Frederick. L. "Negro in the Dance As Katherine Dunham Sees Him." 1938. Rpt. in *Kaiso! Katherine Dunham: An Anthology of Writings.* Ed. VèVè A. Clark and Margaret B. Wilkerson. Berkeley: U of California Institute for the Study of Social Change, 1978. 59–62.

Rose, Albirda. *Dunham Technique: "A Way of Life."* Dubuque: Kendall/Hunt, 1990.

Thomas, Roy. "Focal Rites: New Dance Dominions." *Kaiso! Katherine Dunham: An Anthology of Writings.* Ed. VèVè A. Clark and Margaret B. Wilkerson. Berkeley: U of California Institute for the Study of Social Change, 1978. 112–116.

Wasserman, Dale. "Letter to Katherine Dunham." 31 Dec. 1953. Special Collections. Morris Library, Southern Illinois U, Carbondale.

Williams, Lavinia. "Notations of the Dunham Method and Technique." *Katherine Dunham: Reflections on the Social and Political Contexts of Afro-American Dance.* Ed. Joyce Aschenbrenner. Dance Research Annual XII. New York: CORD, 1981. 121–159.

1   *Bill "Bojangles" Robinson* (left), 1939
     Earl "Snake Hips" Tucker (right), 1938
     Courtesy of Joe Nash Dance Collection
     Schomburg Center, New York Public Library

2 *Hemsley Winfield's*
 New Negro Art Theater Dance Group: "Life and Death"
 Courtesy of Joe Nash Dance Collection
 Schomburg Center, New York Public Library

3 *Rites de Passage*, Lucille Ellis
   Katherine Dunham Collection, Missouri Historical Society, St. Louis
   Courtesy of Katherine Dunham
   Photo by A. Castro, Buenos Aires, 1954

4   *Rehearsal Still "Mambo"*
     Dunham, right foreground
     Mangano, left background
     Katherine Dunham Collection, Missouri Historical Society, St. Louis
     Courtesy of Katherine Dunham
     Photo by Fed. Patelanni, Rome, 1954

5 *Silvana Mangano, "Possession"*
Rehearsal Still, "Mambo"
Katherine Dunham Collection, Missouri Historical Society, St. Louis
Courtesy of Katherine Dunham
Photo by Fed. Patelanni, Rome, 1954

6   *Bebe Miller and Ralph Lemon*
Courtesy of Isaac Julien
Photo by Chelsea Fetzer

7   *Three*
Directed by Isaac Julien, 1999
Dancers: Bebe Miller and Ralph Lemon
Photo courtesy of Isaac Julien and the Victoria Miro Gallery

Isaac Julien
Courtesy of Isaac Julien
Photo by Gordon Brett

8   *"Forming of the Phoenix"*
Dancers from left to right,
front row: Edward Lynch, David (Leo) Hamilton, Merville Jones
back row: Donald Edwards, Vilmore James
Courtesy of The Phoenix Dance Company
Photo by Terry Cryer

(Re)Crossing Borders: The Legacy of Alvin Ailey

Alison D. Goeller

From the beginning of his career until his death in 1989, Alvin Ailey has been something of an enigma in the modern dance world: following in the footsteps of Katherine Dunham and Pearl Primus, Ailey stands as one of the pioneers of modern dance as well as African American concert dance. The list of firsts that his company garnered and continues to garner under the current direction of Judith Jamison is impressive: the first American modern dance company to perform in the Soviet Union since Isadora Duncan (1970); the first black modern dance company to perform at the Metropolitan Opera (1983); and the first modern dance company to make a U.S. government-sponsored tour of the People's Republic of China (1985) (Ailey 7) are among a long list of the Alvin Ailey American Dance Theater's accomplishments. Moreover, his company, at the time of his death in 1989, had performed for more than 15 million people in forty-eight states and forty-five countries on six continents, and they had performed 150 different ballets by more than fifty choreographers (Ailey 6).

Ailey's own numerous awards and commissions testify to the respect he and his company have received over the years: in 1985, he became the first choreographer to be awarded a Distinguished Professorship at City University of New York (Dunning 366); in 1987 he received the Samuel H. Scripps American Dance Festival Award (Dunning 376); and, in 1989, the year he died, he became the youngest artist ever to receive the Kennedy Center Honors (Dunning 383). In addition, over the years, he was commissioned by the Harkness Ballet, the Joffrey Ballet, the American Ballet Theatre, the Paris Opera Ballet, the Royal Danish Ballet, La Scala Opera Ballet, and the Metropolitan Opera Company in New York.

It is clear from the more than fifty dances that Ailey himself choreographed over his lifetime as well as his own comments in interviews and dance notes that at the forefront of his artistic goals was the development of an African American aesthetic in modern dance and also a space within which black dancers and choreographers could freely work without the pressure to conform to racial stereotypes. "My greatest wish," he said in 1969, "is for the black American dancer to enter, through the front door, the mainstream of American dance" (qtd. in DeFrantz 177). Indeed, until Ailey formed his company in 1958, blacks had been either essentially excluded from the world of ballet or segregated, as they were in Agnes de Mille's short-lived "Negro wing" of the American Ballet Theatre, because, it was claimed, their bodies, with their "protruding backsides," were not made for ballet. In 1932, John Martin, dance critic for the *New York Times*, voiced the prevailing attitude about ballet and the black dancer:

> ... its wholly European outlook, history and technical theory are alien to him culturally, temperamentally and anatomically.... In practice there is a racial constant, so to speak, in the proportions of the limbs and torso and the conformation of the feet, all of which affect body placement; in addition, the deliberately maintained erectness of the European dancers's spine is in marked contrast to the fluidity of the Negro dancer's, and the latter's natural concentration of movement in the pelvic region is similarly at odds with European usage. When the Negro takes on the style of the European, he succeeds only in being affected, just as the European dancer who attempts to dance like the Negro seems only gauche. (qtd. in Aschenbrenner 36)

Eight years later, Martin was again to criticize black dancers for "dallying in ballet technique" since African Americans were "not designed to delve into philosophy or psychology but to externalize the impulses of a high-spirited, rhythmic and gracious race" (qtd. in Dixon Gottschild 66). Likewise, in a response to Clive Barnes' attack on him for not using black dancers in his company, George Balanchine, the great Russian ballet master who had immigrated to America in 1934, had also insisted that ballet dancers had "to have a certain kind of build" (Long 118), so he was more than reluctant to use black dancers in his company. When he did, they were segregated in an ensemble of their own and used to present the exotic. Ironically, however, as Balanchine was decrying the black body, his ballets were necessarily absorbing the American culture around him, which, of course, included African American influences. As Brenda Dixon Gottschild has so convincingly pointed out in her book *Digging the Africanist Presence in American Performance: Dance and Other Contexts*, even before Balanchine had immigrated to America he had been open to influences from so-called folk culture: "The groundedness and rhythmic sense that he inherited from the Georgian (Russian) folk dance tradition was the open door that allowed him to embrace the Africanist rhythmic landscape of his adopted homeland" (Dixon Gottschild 63). In addition, his work with Josephine Baker in *Follies* and his choreographic collaboration with Katherine Dunham in the film *Cabin in the Sky* (1940) helped to change Balanchine's outlook and, perhaps more significantly, the face of American ballet forever. Consequently, he was the first American ballet master to employ angular arms, turned in legs, and bent knees in his choreography, all signs of the Africanist influence (Dixon Gottschild 67). Ironically, though Balanchine had felt the black body was not suited for ballet, he actually changed the ideal ballet body from long torso and shorter legs, in vogue in Russian ballet, to short torso and long, long legs. Arthur Mitchell, a black dancer who eventually featured in Balanchine's company and then went on to form the

Dance Theatre of Harlem in 1969, had suggested that this body type really defined the black body:

> There was a fallacy that blacks couldn't do classical ballet – that the bodies were incorrect. But then you talked to Balanchine, who was the great master of them all and changed the look of ballet in the world today. He described his ideal ballerina as having a short torso, long arms, long legs, and a small head. If that's ideal, then we [peoples of African lineage] are perfect. (qtd. in Dixon Gottschild 65)

In contrast to ballet, modern dance, springing as it did out of the anthropological studies of Pearl Primus, Katherine Dunham, Ruth St. Denis and Ted Shawn, was more receptive to using blacks, partly because of their so-called "primitivism." Ruth St. Denis, for instance, had said: "'The Negro is our real dancing teacher. To him it is a vital and necessary thing to dance'" (Long 39). And Ted Shawn, her husband and partner, concurred:

> The Negro has enriched the American dance in every way – ethnic, modern and ballet. They have an extraordinary gift of rhythm, dramatic movement, joyousness, humour, and altogether are racially endowed with dance gifts which place them equal to the Russians, the Spaniards and the Japanese. (qtd. in Aschenbrenner 68)

Unfortunately, such seemingly laudatory comments often implied that black dancers didn't need the rigorous training that white dancers required; it came naturally. On the contrary, Katherine Dunham, in her research of African and Caribbean dances in the 30s and 40s, insisted that these were art forms requiring tremendous discipline and training. Although she recognized that dance was an integral part of life in the communities she studied, it was also a disciplined and learned skill, not something that came naturally.

Ailey, too, in forming his company in 1958 and opening his arms to black dancers denied visibility in the American dance world, wanted to dispel the myth that his dancers just got out there and did what came naturally. As if in response to Balanchine, he tried to deflate the theory that the black body was not suitable for certain kinds of dancing. Taking his lead from Lester Horton, with whom he worked in California early in his career, Ailey pushed the achievements of African American dancers as far as possible and required that his dancers be rigorously trained in ballet, acting, and the modern dance techniques of Martha Graham and Katherine Dunham, among others, as he himself had been. His dancers would do it all. There was also a political agenda hidden in his strategy. As Thomas DeFrantz, the current Ailey archivist, has pointed out: "Versatility long represented survival in core Afro-American culture; Ailey's company required dancers to demonstrate mastery of several forms to confirm a supreme resilience and fly in the face of racist critique" (DeFrantz 86).

Thus, Ailey challenged the mostly segregationist dance world by repeatedly refusing to be labeled as "merely" a black choreographer and employing only black dancers and music. He also refused to stay within the confines of modern dance and even refused to constrain his dancers within strict gender roles. It was this refusal to be clearly defined as this or that kind of choreographer with this or that kind of dance company that was his most important legacy, one that he has passed down to the present Alvin Ailey American Dance Theater and its current director and former dancer, Judith Jamison. Crossing and recrossing the borders of race, aesthetics, and gender, Ailey stands as a major figure in modern as well as postmodern American dance.

Just as Lester Horton, the white choreographer with whom Ailey first worked in California, had employed black dancers in his troupe, so Ailey, at least after his 1962 Far East tour, always had at least one white dancer in his company. In the early years of the company this represented a risk, since, according to Linda Kent, one of his white dancers, he most likely would have received more grants and attention if he hadn't hired whites (Dunning 233). Clive Barnes, the well-known dance critic for the *New York Times*, agreed with Kent. In a 1970 review of *Blues Suite* , one of Ailey's early dances, he wrote:

> Ailey is an equal opportunity employer in a field and at a time when equal opportunity is not that fashionable.... He shows guts as an administrator ... and that same gutsy quality emerges in his choreography. It would be easier – more acceptable – for Ailey to form an all-Black company, for then, as the obvious black leader in American dance, guilty foundations would have to beat a path to his door. But Ailey goes the hard way of his conscience. (qtd. in Dunning 253)

Moreover, Ailey made few racial distinctions when he assigned parts, refusing to see color onstage. Responding to a claim made by Agnes de Mille that black dancers in a Texas musical were historically inappropriate, he loudly declared in his autobiography that:

> What we're talking about here is dance. We're talking about fantasy, not reality. We're in the theater, not in a history seminar. It's the same as saying that Japanese dancers can't dance the blues – well, they do in my company. Japanese dancers understand the blues as well as anybody. (qtd. in Ailey 128)

Ailey also felt that a mixed company universalized his dances; consequently, minority white dancers performed the same dances as the African American majority. Linda Kent, for instance, a white dancer, regularly performed roles that portrayed Africans or African Americans: in *The Wedding* (1961), a piece based on Pearl Primus' research of African and Caribbean dance and ritual, Kent played the sister of the bride; and in the "Move, Members, Move" section of *Revelations*, she often played the "Bible thumping, fanwagging black matron" who organizes the church women (Dunning 253).

Quintet, a dance Ailey created in 1968 about a Motown female singing group, is another good example of Ailey's refusal to pigeonhole his dancers into roles based on their skin color. Featuring four black dancers and one white dancer, all wearing blonde wigs, tight dresses, and high heels and dancing to the voice of white blues singer Laura Nyro, *Quintet* confused racial boundaries, while at the same time critiquing them. It thus became a kind of mock minstrel, with blacks imitating whites imitating blacks and one white woman imitating a black imitating a white, thereby exposing the absurdity of categories. What was more important to Ailey, however, was conveying the tension between the public and private lives of celebrities, black or white, and this he accomplished through a contrast of movement styles. As Thomas DeFrantz describes it, when the five dancers performed together, their bold, expansive movements suggested the glamour of stardom; but when they performed their solos, they discarded their stage costumes and moved with often agonizing gestures, falling to the floor or swaggering in arhythmic hesitations to suggest their disillusionment with their public lives. Kent's solo movements, a combination of Graham and Horton technique, contrasted with the black social dances that were performed by the rest of the dancers; but it was the difference in Kent's movements, not in her skin color, that served as a metaphor for alienation and isolation from the group (DeFrantz 151–155).

Ailey's *Pas de Duke* (1976) is another piece that shows the choreographer's willingness to cross and recross racial borders. Hailed as the "meeting of two worlds" (qtd. in DeFrantz 272), the duet featured Mikhail Baryshnikov, a short, white classical ballet dancer from Russia and Judith Jamison, a 5'10" black American female modern dancer, performing to the music of Duke Ellington. In order to challenge the audience's expectations and assumptions, Ailey designed the piece so that Jamison, primarily a modern dancer, performed many of the traditonal balletic movements, while Baryshnikov, a classical ballet dancer, strutted and moved in often funky, jazzy ways, apparently a challenge to the Russian, who was accustomed to an erect spine and torso. Thus the dance offered an array of dynamic contrasts: race, gender, nationality, technical background, and physical stature (DeFrantz 272). It was as if Ailey were declaring to the dance world: boundaries, labels, mean very little; look what's possible when even the most seemingly incongruous elements are joined together. "We talk too much of black art," Ailey once said in an interview, "when we should be talking about art, just art...." Color should be "an irrelevant factor in the world of dance" (qtd. in DeFrantz 142).

Katherine Dunham had earlier expressed the same philosophy and had run into opposition from the government over her integrated company; but by the late 60's and early 70's the U.S. State Department, with pressure from the Civil Rights Movement, had changed course, and Ailey's company was consistently chosen by them as cultural ambassadors, touring over forty-five countries in the years he was the director. Presumably, his "carefully integrated roster of artists presented a liberal American philosophy of racial equity and harmony" that the State Department was eager to present to the world (DeFrantz 120).

Although Ailey centered many of his most well-known works, such as *Blues Suite* and *Revelations*, around themes from his own childhood in Texas, what he called "blood memories," he also choreographed dances that were not specific to his own African American heritage. Ballets like *Mistress and Manservant* (1959), based on Strindberg's *Miss Julie*; *Knoxville Summer of 1915* (1960), based on James Agee's *A Death in the Family*; *Hermit Songs* (1961), based on early Irish poems, *Labyrinth* (1963), based on the story of Theseus and the Minotaur; *The Twelve Gates* (1964), based on images of women in the Bible; *Riedaglia* (1971), a dance about the seven deadly sins; *Flowers* (1971), his work dealing with the death of rock stars from drugs; *Lark Ascending* (1972), a tribute to the Scottish countryside; and *Hidden Rites* (1973) all made it clear that Ailey was committed to producing a full range of material that would challenge both his choreographic abilities as well as those of his dancers.

Along with his insistence upon an integrated dance company and a wide range of subject matter was Ailey's refusal to be bound by aesthetic categories, crossing and recrossing the lines separating ballet, modern dance, tap, musical theater, and so-called ethnic/folk dancing. Having come to dance originally through a combination of his athletic interests, particularly gymnastics and football, and visits to performances of the Ballet Russe de Monte Carlo and Katherine Dunham's all-black *Tropical Review* when he was still in high school in California, Ailey was probably destined to become an eclectic choreographer. When he left California in 1954 with Carmen de Lavallade to perform in *House of Flowers* on Broadway, he met and studied under nearly all the important modern dance teachers at the time: Doris Humphrey, Charles Weidman, Hanya Holme, Martha Graham, and Katherine Dunham, absorbing each of their particular techniques. His short-lived time as an actor on Broadway, later his work with George Balanchine, and his opera commissions in Paris, Milan and New York helped fuel his wide-ranging style. In addition, his tours in Asia, Africa, and Australia literally had him crossing and recrossing borders. He also read widely and took notes when he traveled and insisted that his dancers be widely-read as well. Moreover, Ailey employed a range of musical styles to accompany his dances: pop music, jazz, blues, spirituals, opera, classical music, African drum beats. Indeed, at a time in modern dance history when, as Jennifer Dunning puts it, "solemn choreography performed by blank-faced dancers was largely the fashion in modern dance" (110), Ailey challenged the prevailing aesthetic with his lively hybridity and his theatricality.

Ailey also provided a space for other choreographers. Bill T. Jones, for instance, the well-known postmodern choreographer, was given his first commercial opportunity with Ailey's company, and Ailey also helped launch the careers of such diverse choreographers as Ulysses Dove, Donald McKayle, Talley Beatty, and, of course, Judith Jamison. As he said in an interview in 1986, Ailey felt it was crucial to his company and also to the dance world that young choreographers be given space and opportunity to see their work performed ("Evening"). Judith Jamison has continued Ailey's work with her recent Women's Choreographic Initiative and her encouragement of such artists as Jawole Willa Jo Zoller ("Alvin Ailey," Interview).

Unfortunately, Ailey's eclecticism often led to charges that his work was too commercial, too "show bizzy, " wasn't black enough or artsy enough or was selling out to white audiences. By 1974, Arlene Croce, a respected dance critic, wondered if his success resulted not from his artistry but from its "multiracial character, its native populism, its ecumenical repertory ... as a cause for good liberal Americans" (qtd. in DeFrantz 174). But Anna Kisselgoff, in an essay that appeared in the *New York Times* in 1978, entitled "Has Ailey Really Gone Commerical," defended Ailey in this way:

> The broad appeal of the Ailey company should not be confused with Broadway's policy of presenting works out of box office considerations instead of an artist's need to express himself creatively. In fact, the record shows that Alvin Ailey has given more young choreographers – including black choreographers who have not had this wide an audience – a greater chance than any artistic director of a major company.... An artistic director who allows so many choreographers to express themselves – to fail as often as they succeed – is a very odd commercial specimen. (qtd. in Dunning 340–41)

Ailey wanted dance to be accessible to his audiences, adamant that his dances appeal to a wide black as well as white audience. "That's my perception of what dance should be," he said in his autobiography," a popular form, wrenched from the hands of the elite" (Ailey 101). "Dance came from the people," he said in a 1986 interview, "and it should be delivered back to the people" ("Evening"). In fact, Ailey was not ashamed of the "show-biz" quality of much of his work. As he himself said in another interview, "We're also show-biz. And I'm not ashamed of that. Black people have had a long tradition of that, and it's one of the things we, as a company, do very well" (qtd. in DeFrantz 161).

Finally, Ailey crossed gender boundaries by challenging gender stereotypes and redefining gender imagery. Although he never admitted publically his homosexuality and disliked any hint of femininity in his male dancers, at least some of his choreographed pieces, especially the later ones, do hint at what Thomas DeFrantz calls "an elusive bond between gay men" (303). *Streams*, for instance, a plotless ballet he created in 1980 and still in the Ailey repertoire, includes several same sex partners, as well as heterosexual couples, performing identical movements, challenging the audience ever so subtly and gently to consider the possibility of homosexual love, although Anna Kisselgoff, in reviewing the piece, noted that "the final plea for all kinds of love – both heterosexual and homosexual – is stated so subtly that many might miss the message" (qtd. in DeFrantz 303). Ailey's willingness to cross gender lines, if ever so carefully, has continued in the company. Speaking of his work in an all-male cast of *Shelter*, a piece originally about homeless women, dancer Guillermo Asca has said recently:

> ... when a man loses his home, his job, it's more of a desperate situation and the man loses respect for himself, and it just became this almost more powerful piece to me and to perform it was overwhelming.... It created just such a bond within the men just to get through this piece and the emotions were always overwhelming dancing it. ("Alvin Ailey," Interview)

Moreover, the lifelong influence of Ailey's very strong and loving mother, the close working relationship he had with Judith Jamison, a dancer of enormous power, both physically and emotionally, and the fact that modern dance from its inception had been dominated by women most likely contributed to Ailey's refusal to give in to traditional gender roles in creating his dances, as is apparent in a dance like *Pas De Duke*, where Ailey challenges the classic balletic tradition of the delicate ballerina supported by the athletic and stronger male by juxtaposing the tall and dynamic Jamison beside a much shorter Baryshnikov. *Cry*, another dance he created in 1971 for Judith Jamison and dedicated to "all black women everywhere, and especially our mothers" (Jamison 134), illustrates Ailey's interest in creating strong female roles. A fifteen-minute solo, the dance essentially takes us through the history of the black American woman, from her experiences on the auction block, through her duties as a slave, to the joys and sorrows of being a mother. But rather than focus on her weaknesses and the burdens she cannot bear, her strength overwhelms her sorrows. Jamison herself has said that *Cry* is about "triumphing after all the madness ... with head held high" and, in fact, in every ballet she did for Ailey there was a strong female leader ("Evening"). In *Revelations* her role as the deaconess, proudly carrying a large white umbrella and dominating the space around her, underlined the incredible power and energy of Ailey's female dancers, especially when she was juxtaposed beside a dancer like Dudley Williams, who exuded a much gentler, softer presence on stage.

A closer look at Ailey's most popular and well-known dance, *Revelations*, first performed on January 31, 1960, at the 92nd Street Y in New York and still the company's most popular dance, is perhaps the best way of summarizing Ailey's extraordinary ability to cross and recross borders, to blend a wide range of aesthetic and thematic elements into a pleasing whole. Although the suite is clearly a tribute to black culture and in particular black religious music, from the sorrow songs and spirituals to blues and gospel rock, its dizzying mix of classical ballet steps, Graham technique, Dunham-styled island rhythms and movements, jazz and Broadway musical dance is testament to Ailey's genius for hybridity. And his consistent foregrounding of powerful female dancers, both physically and emotionally, illustrates his determination to resist gender stereotyping. Although the suite has transformed itself with each new generation of dancers, its basic format has remained unchanged after forty years. The suite consists of three major parts: "Pilgrim of Sorrow," where the darkly-lit stage introduces the theme of the need and search for salvation; "Take Me to the Water," where the reenactment of a baptismal ceremony, with the by-now famous Ailey props, suggests a move toward redemption; and "Move, Members, Move," a piece set in a country church, employing a full cast of dancers and an upbeat, hopeful, and highly theatrical finale.

In "I've Been 'Buked," the opening piece in the first section, the dancers are grouped closely together, as if to support one another as they simultaneously bend their knees in classic Graham fashion, slowly and precisely, upper bodies stiff, arms angular. As the dancers' weight is pushed down towards the floor, the deep knee bends indicate rootedness in this life, the life of the body with all its worldly woes. But when they stretch upwards, with open palms, their humility before God and, perhaps more importantly, their faith that there will be relief from the sorrows of their lives is made clear. At times their movements are jagged, abrupt, a sign of precariousness and lack of assuredness. In contrast, the next piece, "Didn't My Lord Deliver Daniel," picks up the pace as the dancers contract their torsos and pelvises, again borrowing from Graham, roll their heads as if in a frenzy, and employ the Dunham technique of body isolation, that is, moving different parts of their bodies to different rhythms. The dancers end on the floor, with much of their weight on their shoulders, perhaps again suggesting their precarious spiritual position. "Fix Me, Jesus," the next piece, and the last one in the first section, is a traditional balletic pas de deux, with the male supporting the female in slow lifts and extensions and with traditional ballet arms. The rhythm and movement convey a feeling of floating, as the dancers are calling for help from Jesus. But here we also see evidence of what Brenda Dixon Gottschild has identified as the Africanist presence as the female dancer is almost always slightly off balance, nearly falling to the floor at times.

In the second section of *Revelations*, the mood and scene shift to a more specific, less abstract scene: the river and the baptismal ceremony. In "Honor, Honor," a transitional piece, the Ailey props are introduced: a large white umbrella, long, white streamers flowing from nearly ceiling-high poles, and long, flowing sheer scarves, adding theatricality to the dance and suggesting that a baptism in water is about to be performed. The use of props is continued in the next piece, "Wade in the Water," one of the most well-known segments of *Revelations*. Here, in "Africanist" style, the dancers swagger on stage, leading with their hips, a marked contrast to classical ballet's insistence upon an erect torso and tucked-in derriere, where the center of a dancer's body is the spine, and all movement, whether leg lifts or turns, extends from there. The isolated shoulder movements are also notable. On the one hand, the dancers move their shoulders in what looks very much like the Haitian "zepaules," a basic dance movement in vaudoun practice that Dunham identified in her research. And the undulating motion of their spines likewise could be in imitation of a dance honoring Damballa, the Haitian snake god. But then quite naturally, and as a fascinating contrast, these movements lead into a classical "waving" motion of the arms and classical bourée steps that easily remind one of the arms of the dying swan in *Swan Lake*. Again, in contrast, the dancers occasionally roll on the floor and even walk on their knees; according to Dixon Gottschild, this is an Africanist aesthetic: the dancers "get down" close to the earth (14).

In the only solo of *Revelations*, "I Want to Be Ready," one again notices a range of movements and styles: floor work typical of the Graham technique, the Africanist influence in the form of precarious balancing and pelvic contractions, as well as elements of ballet and musical theater. Much of the time the dancer's feet are planted flat on the ground, emphasizing his weight and the pull of gravity; but the soloist also performs on the floor, presumably to indicate his humility before God but also to show his struggle, as he works against gravity, to "be ready." There is also a great deal of holding and releasing tension, particularly in his abdomen. To add to the hybridity of the piece, ballet arabesques are used; however, instead of suggesting stability, as they would in a classical dance, they imply stylized instability and precariousness as we see in some of the earlier segments. To relieve the tension of "I Want To Be Ready, " the last piece in the second section, "Sinner Man," is highly athletic, in fact, the most athletic piece of the suite, employing three male dancers who run, jump, turn, and slide, as if attempting to avoid punishment for the sins of this world.

The freneticism of "Sinner Man" leads nicely into the third and final section of *Revelations,* the fast-paced and short "You May Run On," and is followed by the highly theatrical finale, "Rocka My Soul," where props are again used to add color as well as specificity to the dance: the wooden stools and fans easily suggest the interior of any one of those black churches that Ailey attended as a child in Texas and that he often singled out as the most important aspect of the black community ("Alvin Ailey," CD). The props as well as the women's movements add a comic touch new to the suite as the women furiously fan themselves while dancing from a seated position on their stools. When their male counterparts enter, we see most clearly Ailey's love for classical jazz and Broadway musical theater as the men, hands on hips, swagger across the stage and the women stand on their stools, chiding the men to be good Christians. The final moments of *Revelations* are pure Broadway, and the audience is left envigorated and inspired.

To conclude, I would like to suggest that Ailey's legacy of hybridity, although certainly not entirely new, enjoyed a success unequalled in American dance

theater. Following in the footsteps of Dunham and other pioneers, his eclecti-
cism has become a kind of metaphor for the country and its people he so loved.
Appropriating and reappropriating elements from various cultures and disci-
plines, Ailey was able to exploit the almost limitless variety that we call the
American landscape. Refusing to be bound by race and gender, Ailey passed on
his genius to other dance companies like the Dallas Black Dance Theatre, the
Dayton Contemporary Dance Company, Denver's Cleo Parker Robinson Dance
Company, the Philadelphia Dance Company, and Lula Washington's Los Angeles Contemporary Dance Theatre (DeFrantz 148). Perhaps the clearest testament to his greatness as an artist and as a liberator of the black body is the
company's longevity: under Judith Jamison the company has just celebrated its
fortieth anniversary and there is every indication that it will continue to inspire a
wide-range of its public in the new millenium.

Works Cited

Ailey, Alvin with A. Peter Bailey. *Revelations.* Secaucus, NJ: Citadel Press, 1995.
Alvin Ailey American Dance Theater: A Musical Retrospective on Forty Years of Dance.
    The Alvin Ailey American Dance Theater Foundation, CD, 1998.
"Alvin Ailey American Dance Theater." Interview. By Dorothea Fischer-
    Hornung and Alison D. Goeller: Baden-Baden, 12 Oct. 1999.
Aschenbrenner, Joyce. ed. *Katherine Dunham: Reflections on the Social and Political
    Contexts of Afro-American Dance.* Dance Research Annual XII. New York:
    CORD, 1981.
DeFrantz, Thomas. "'Revelations': The Choreographies of Alvin Ailey." Diss.
    New York U, 1997.
Dixon Gottschild, Brenda. *Digging the Africanist Presence in American Performance:
    Dance and Other Contexts.* Westport, CT: Greenwood Press, 1996.
Dunning, Jennifer. *Alvin Ailey: A Life in Dance.* New York: Da Capo Press, 1996.
"Evening with the Alvin Ailey American Dance Theater." Dance Video. 1986.
Jamison, Judith with Howard Kaplan. *Dancing Spirit: An Autobiography.* New
    York: Doubleday, 1993.
Long, Richard. *The Black Tradition in American Dance.* New York: Rizzoli, 1989.

Phoenix Perspectives: African American Influences on a British Dance Company

Christy Adair

Introduction

In the video clip of Phoenix Dance Company's *Forming of the Phoenix* (1982), choreographed by Leo Hamilton, we see the performers dance to music by Aswad, Britain's top reggae band. They set up scenes of the everyday, of meeting each other, slapping hands, arrivals and departures. *Forming of the Phoenix*, as the title suggests, tells the story of how the company began and, with evident parody, highlights individual characteristics and styles of each dancer (see Illus. 8). Leo Hamilton is introduced as the person who initiated the idea of the group, and, as well as being interested in modern dance, he is also a martial arts expert; Villmore James is introduced as the comedian of the group; Merville Jones as the ballet dancer; Donald Edwards is seen skanking – performing his version of a Charlie Chaplin walk – and the toasting or rapping commentary by Edward Lynch gives the verbal context of the company's beginning. Hamilton said of the piece, "On the surface it's about how the group was formed. The interaction of the people make up the group. Behind that is the core of the idea which is, like the mythical bird itself, taking from itself to develop, it dies and everything takes place within itself" (Holgate 14). There is, therefore, within the company, a continuous process of renewal and rejuvenation.

So how do I discuss this company? It is part of British modern dance culture, and yet it is frequently labeled as a "black dance" company. What is evident in the work of Phoenix is their contribution to a dance lineage which has tended to marginalize the contributions of people of African descent. Through discussion of their work, it is possible to reconsider perceptions of, and influences on, British modern dance.

In postmodernity reconsiderations of ways of thinking about diversity, identity and agency are evident. The concept of agency is complex, but one aspect of it is the resistance to codes and structures of gender and cultural difference. Within dance performance there are opportunities to play with notions of identities through physicality and to present resistance to preconceived ideas of gender and cultural difference. In this paper I will discuss the establishment of Phoenix Dance Company in relation to these issues together with some of the African American influences upon the company.

The company established themselves as a contemporary dance company drawing on their understanding of Laban's theories of movement, Graham technique and popular club culture.[1] However, the response to their work, throughout the company's eighteen-year history, has frequently been about the composition of the company, as initially all the dancers were male and of African/Caribbean descent, so that they have been viewed as a "black dance" company and positioned as signifying cultural difference. The dilemma for both the company and for spectators is valuing the particular without physical signs of difference being read as otherness and a site for discriminatory readings.

Unfortunately, there are many examples, particularly in the media, of attempts to acknowledge and value difference but which instead reinscribe it. This is certainly the case with the use of the term "black," which I discuss later. However, both the background and the composition of the company, together with the positive response to the dancing and the repertoire from critics and audience, made Phoenix legendary. These factors also ensured that the company moved from a small-scale, independent company to an Arts-Council-funded company just four years after it was established.

As the company had minimal formal training, they received little exposure to the African American influences that they might be expected to draw upon as modern dancers, for example, Katherine Dunham and Alvin Ailey. Indeed, even with training it is possible that they would not have been introduced to these significant artists, as the traditional approaches to dance history have tended to ignore African American contributions to modern dance. The African American influences they were inspired by were musicians and dancers who could be seen on film, such as the Nicholas Brothers. The importance of these latter artists is evident in the statement of one writer in the *New Yorker* who claimed that "practically every move in breakdancing, however new it may look, is not just foreshadowed but completely expressed in what the Nicholas Brothers did (Emery 360). Indeed, as ballet star Baryshnikov suggests, we can recognize their style in break dancing and rap. Also, of course, from MTV and TV programs rap and break dancing can be seen all over the world where people adopt it and make it their own. It is also an aspect of the club culture Phoenix drew upon.

My focus on this company comes from my interest in developing my earlier writing on women and dance and my role as a lecturer in Leeds in a degree program at the Northern School of Contemporary Dance, which has many close connections with the company. I think it is important to discuss dance as a part of contemporary culture and at the same time to recognize my own cultural and gender position as a white female. The dilemma, of course, is how to acknowledge and examine categories related to postmodernity and cultural difference without fixing meaning. In discussing this work there is the danger of misunder-

---

[1]   In Britain the term contemporary dance is frequently used instead of modern dance.

standing cultural references or of perceiving issues from a viewpoint which is narrowed by an imperialist gaze. However, it seems crucial to write about these histories and issues and to avoid what hooks describes as the representation of blackness as one-dimensional, based on "colonial imperialist paradigms" (28) and which reinforces and sustains white supremacy.

It seems appropriate, in the context of rapid change in relation to diversity, to readdress the balance of research, particularly in light of contemporary events in Britain. For example, the Windrush Season was a year of events to celebrate the arrival of the Empire Windrush at Tilbury on 22 June 1948. This ship carried 500 men and women from the Caribbean, now regarded as the founders of the country's black community, who together with their descendants have significantly shaped British culture (Phillips and Phillips 6).

Another significant event providing evidence of cultural change is the report from the inquiry into the murder of Stephen Lawrence, described in the press as a "black teenager." This report concluded that police mishandled the case because of incompetence and institutional racism. This latter term, after much controversy and debate, was defined by Sir William Macpherson as "the collective failure of an organization to provide an appropriate and professional service to people because of their color, culture or ethnic origin" (Travis 1). This has far reaching implications for other British institutions. It appears, therefore, that the understanding of issues of identity, agency and diversity are on the agenda in Britain. Moreover, the climate may be right for the artistic and structural changes which the current artistic director of Phoenix Dance Company, Thea Barnes, wants to see put in place.

It is appropriate to ensure that Phoenix has a prominent place in the history of modern dance in Britain rather than in the marginalized box labeled "black dance." This label, I have argued elsewhere, has been useful politically, but it is problematic to use the term "black" without being fixed by binary oppositions (Adair 162). In addition, it has been argued that "the universal application of "black" as a concept lacks cultural historical specificity" (Brooks 16). It is a generic term applied in Britain to people who share an experience of slavery and racism and in this sense it is still widely used, and in a British context it is difficult to avoid. In an interview with dance critic Judith Mackrell, Thea Barnes stated that it is now time to get rid of the "b" word (See Mackrell 12–13). However, Mackrell acknowledges the paradox that in Britain "black" still has a live function, and for Phoenix black remains part of its public identity – if only because black or mostly black groups are rare here in Britain. But as Barnes points out, no one really knows what a black company means other than some mish mash of stereotypes about movement and people's duties (See Makrell 12–13). Despite this, there is growing recognition of the contribution of African American culture to modern and postmodern dance which now needs to be considered further.

Company Contextual History

Modern dance in Britain evolved from a number of pioneers, including Laban, and from an American dance tradition of Graham technique as it was taught at the London School of Contemporary Dance. In the current reconsiderations of modernism, the recognition that African American contributions have been denied, hidden and/or appropriated is being foregrounded (Dixon Gottschild 1991: 15). In America, as Thomas DeFrantz states, "Modern dance allowed for more fluid connections between the dancing body, cultural representation, and dance technique, and the post-World War II era saw a number of dancers and choreographers working to redefine the black male presence on the concert stage" (112). Although these changes did not directly affect the work of Phoenix, they are the wider context in which their work took place.

Throughout the seventies there was a thriving and developing dance culture mainly based in London. By the early eighties, dance was disseminated more widely and modern and new dance were coming of age in Britain. In Leeds, Phoenix's hometown, exposure to modern dance was predominantly through the performances and residencies of visiting companies. But the impetus for Phoenix's beginnings was not the theatrical dance culture but the club culture of the late seventies and early eighties. There were numerous difficulties for the African Caribbean community in a society which did not welcome those who were viewed as "different." So they made their own entertainment and began their own clubs. Many African Caribbean people, particularly young men, were unemployed; therefore, when Donald Edwards, Villmore James and Leo Hamilton decided that they wanted to start a dance company, they were making the decision from a background of entrepreneurial skills, knowing that their employment possibilities were strictly limited.

The Company

Rejuvenation is certainly a theme for the company, but the struggle has been for agency, rather than being driven by funders and critics. As one critic noted:

> If you call yourself Phoenix everyone wants to re-invent you, and under various directors the company has switched from being emphatically all male to emphatically mixed gender: it has gone from all black to mixed race and back again. While its identity has been agonized over, the repertory has often been left hanging. (Craine 9)

Initially, the company performed locally, as they firmly believed in taking dance into the community where they developed a strong following. The company was

small scale with no aspirations to become anything else. Their style was a mixture of contemporary and reggae dance styles, influenced by the community
from which it came. Music such as reggae, jazz and calypso contributed and
projected itself through the company's work (Holgate 9). They presented a
strong positive image in contrast to the negative images in the media of riots
and stereotypes of violence of young, Caribbean/British men.

Their youthful energy gripped audiences when they performed in London,
and, despite a heavy touring schedule with poor resources, their reputation grew.
While the company perceived themselves as a local company, they also had a
national profile as part of the youth dance movement. When they performed
alongside their old school's youth group at national festivals, they were very well
received. After their performances in London in February 1983, one critic described them saying:

> Phoenix Dance Company looked impressively different. They danced with con-
> viction and muscular ease. They had put together choreography that was musical
> and showed them off well and they had not forgotten that theatre dance takes
> place in a theatre and has to please, impress and extend an audience's imagina-
> tion (Dromgoole qtd. in Holgate 12).

There was a TV documentary made about them for the prestigious South Bank
Show in November 1984. By this time they were considered to be a good example of what could be achieved outside London. The turning point for the company was when they were cited in an Arts Council Report, *Glory of the Garden*
(1984), as having the qualities and criteria for funding which the Arts Council
proposed. Up until April 1985 Phoenix was a limited company; in 1986 they
moved into permanent premises at the Yorkshire Dance Centre. Clearly, the
company established themselves very quickly, and the conditions for the dancers
changed dramatically from a cooperative, small-scale venture to a nationally recognized organization with a management board.

Repertoire - The Forming of the Phoenix

One of the issues to be addressed when considering the repertoire of Phoenix is
how art can be made which values and recognizes particular and common
bonds, while at the same time resisting the distorting labels and categories which
are imposed in societies which are marred by asymmetries of power. For example, Blondell Cummings, who is an African American choreographer, refers to
this issue in her discussion of being disturbed by an insistence on viewing her
work only in terms of her "race." This is, of course, an issue for many perform-

ers and companies, who are defined as "black," including Phoenix (Cooper Albright 195).

This is a theme which Susan Manning raises in her discussion of American modern dance in the thirties. She states that white choreographers cast white dancers as metaphorical Native Americans and African Americans in a context of predominantly white spectatorship. However, with the development of black spectatorship, choreographers concentrated on presenting "visions of blackness" rather than exploring "the potential of the black body to represent whiteness ... so the underlying representational trope remained: whereas the white body could represent a universal body, the black body could represent only a black body" (192–93). In addition, of course, as scholar Brenda Dixon Gottschild points out, "Too often the black dancing body has become the screen upon which untenable fantasies are projected: it can be an object of love or scorn, admiration or ridicule, emancipation or repression – that is, the battlefield where binary opposites are played out" (1991: 16).

The early Phoenix repertoire choreographed by company members was concerned with exploring elements of cultural experiences which were important to them, from sources as varied as club culture, martial arts, films and family. For many critics and for some audiences this was interpreted as "visions of blackness." The legend of Phoenix was partly created by the 1984 TV documentary and a piece entitled *The Forming of the Phoenix* (1982). This legend is a story of five socially disadvantaged young men in eighties Britain making good. Their style was described as "very much butch-matey, jokey-sporty athletic, streetdance contemporary, but with strands of reference to social issues of race and color that united the dancers and their public peers" (Dougill).

In the 1984 TV documentary the dancers make clear that for them dancing is a central, integral part of their lives and that they do not separate their club experiences from their stage and touring experiences. They enjoy dancing and want to share that with a range of people through workshops and performances on tour. Their work is an example of Cooper Albright's consideration of the "ways in which the performing body physicalizes the autobiographical voice to produce a representation of subjectivity which is at once whole and fragmented" (182).

However, this is frequently overlooked by critics and writers who, while recognizing that the company is dynamic, powerful and highly original, still assume that the work is about a one-dimensional view of what it means to be "black." Such views reinforce essentialism. For example, one critic's article was headlined "Where Did the Blackness Go?" (Dromgoole). In contrast, Brenda Dixon Gottschild (1996) argues against such a limited perspective and introduces the concept of an Africanist aesthetic. She suggests that there is a difference between what she terms European-based aesthetics and African-based aesthetics. For example, in the latter, one part of the body is played against other body parts. This example can be seen in Dunham's work, which offered a vocabulary which had previously been hidden and denied.

As hooks states, "The critique of essentialism encouraged by postmodernist thought is useful for African Americans concerned with reformulating out-moded notions of identity. We have too long had imposed upon us from both the outside and the inside a narrow, constricting notion of blackness" (28). She also says that such a critique allows affirmation of multiple black identities and varied black experiences which is clearly pertinent when considering the work of Phoenix whether past, present or future.

What is, unfortunately, evident in examples of critics' writings from the eighties and through the nineties is the expectations of the predominantly white European critical establishment for performers of African descent to be the repository and expressers of "race" almost as though, as Paul Gilroy points out, "The history of slavery is somehow assigned to blacks. It becomes our special property rather than a part of the ethical and intellectual heritage of the West as a whole" (49).

In the readings of the work of Phoenix it is important to take into account the view that modern subjectivity is fractured, multiple and decentered rather than limiting the potential of the work by assuming a unified subject. To some extent *Forming of the Phoenix* (1982) and *Nightlife at the Flamingo* (1983) illustrate the drive for agency in contrast to the one-dimensional negative images of black masculinity portrayed in the media. Phoenix was and is a successful modern dance company and is one of the few surviving repertory dance companies in Britain today. Initially, as an early program states, they did not "consider them-selves just as dancers," as all members also choreographed. This is probably a tribute to their early educational experiences in schools where making work was as important as performing it. They were described as stretching themselves and their audiences by producing work which ranged from ritual to comedy, from autobiography to imagination and used music from UB40 to Berlioz. (*Dance Umbrella*) *Nightlife at the Flamingo* (1983) is set in an imaginary American nightclub in the thirties. The work is energetic and exuberant, integrating popular culture with modern dance. The work was noted as one of the most popular pieces in the early repertoire and contains a fast-moving duet, reminiscent of the work of the Nicholas Brothers. The dance is a mixture of lindy hop, tap and modern dance, creating rhythmic connections between each other. The atmosphere is highly charged, and the performers are shown having a good time, emphasized by unison and, on occasions, rhythmic clapping.

The duet in *Nightlife at the Flamingo* is modelled on a duet previously per-formed by the Nicholas Brothers, with spins, jumps and razzmatazz showman-ship; there is dancing on the table and a sense of unstoppability. Edward Lynch, one of the dancers and the choreographer of the piece, said that he wanted the dancers to "just dance to the music without counts.... That's how I saw it.

American dancers went to the disco and just went to enjoy it" (qtd. in Evans). The video clip shows dancers in a dance hall in the forties, mostly African Americans, juxtaposed with the Phoenix dancers in a local club. Lynch talks about a happy atmosphere and not training for dance, just doing it. In this statement he links social and theatrical dance, which is an important element of some of the Phoenix repertoire. However, by ignoring the dance rehearsals involving numerous repetitions of dance repertoire and training systems which the dancers are committed to – for example, Leo Hamilton studied karate – he reinforces the stereotype that black dancers dance naturally. He has internalized the stereotype and, therefore, does not acknowledge that learning dance is part of a process either from a social setting, from more formal dance training, or from both.

The Nicholas Brothers

The inspiration for the work came from the Nicholas Brothers, acknowledged as one of the greatest dance teams ever known; their career spanned over sixty years. They performed at the Cotton Club in Harlem, a showcase for top African American artists in the twenties and thirties. However, although African Americans were employed both as artists and support staff, they were not allowed in as audience. On a documentary program about the dancers, it was suggested that when people talked about Fred Astaire and Gene Kelly, they did not mention the Nicholas Brothers because of racism (Bould and Martin). That combined with scarcity of work led to the Nicholas Brothers, like many other African American artists, going to Europe, as there were more opportunities.

In Harlem, white people came to watch the black dancers and Langston Hughes wrote:

> The lindy-hoppers at the Savoy even began to practice acrobatic routines, and to do absurd things for the entertainment of the whites, that probably never would have entered their heads to attempt merely for their own effortless amusement. Some of the lindy-hoppers had cards printed with their names on them and became dance professors teaching the tourists. (qtd. in Emery 222)

Conclusion

Today, performers of African descent have access to less confining contexts. However, the debate about labeling work of the performers, for example the much disputed term "black dance," and the quest for artists to make the work they find engaging without enduring closed response, is ongoing within contemporary British dance culture. In addition, the power of the critics and the ways in which they reinforce inappropriate notions of identity are frequently challenged.

For both the early and the later Phoenix, issues of agency and cultural difference are important aspects of their work. The early Phoenix drew on aspects of their identities as African Caribbean young men who were also British. They evolved their work from their enjoyment of, and inspiration from club culture, part of which evolved from African American influences. They performed this element of their work with relaxed, flowing physicalities together with the stretched lines, strength and momentum gained from Graham technique. Currently, Thea Barnes is contributing to the development of the company as she confidently draws on African and African American traditions and articulates the appropriateness of the Phoenix contribution to the development of dance culture. Her vision and direction for the company neither deny blackness nor are confined by it. However, how Phoenix evolves will depend as much upon the openness of critics and funders and their willingness to support innovative practice within the company as it does upon Barnes' artistic vision. These are some of the elements of the current renewal and rejuvenation of the Phoenix Dance Company as it takes its place in the history and culture of modern dance in Britain.

Works Cited

Adair, Christy. *Women and Dance: Sylphs and Sirens.* London: Macmillan, 1992.

Arts Council of Great Britain. *Glory of the Garden,* 1984.

Bould, Chris, and Michael Martin, Dirs. *We Sing, We Dance: The Nicholas Brothers.* Channel 4, 1992.

Brooks, Ann. *Postfeminisms: Feminism, Cultural Theory and Cultural Forms.* London: Routledge, 1997.

Cooper Albright, Ann. "Auto-Body Stories: Blondell Cummings and Autobiography in Dance." *Meaning in Motion.* Ed. Jane Desmond. Durham: Duke UP, 1997. 179–202.

Craine, Debra. "Dance: Phoenix." *The Guardian* 28 Apr. 1998: 9.

Dance Umbrella Festival Borshure, 1985.

DeFrantz, Thomas. "Simmering Passivity: The Black Male Body in Concert Dance." *Moving Words.* Ed. Gay Morris. London: Routledge, 1996. 107–120.

Dixon Gottschild, Brenda. "The Afrocentric Paradigm." *Design for Arts in Education* Jan./Feb. 1991: 15–22.

—. *Digging the Africanist Presence in American Performance: Dance and Other Contexts.* Westport, CT: Green-wood P, 1996.

Dougill, David. "At Spring Loaded: David Dougill Encounters the Highs and Lows of Contemporary Dance." *Sunday Times* 3 May, 1998: 24.

Dromgoole, Nicholas. "Where Did the Blackness Go?" *Sunday Telegraph* 16 June, 1996: 8.

Emery, Lynne Fauley. *Black Dance from 1619 to Today.* London: Dance Books, 1988.

Evans, Kim. Dir. *The South Bank Show: Phoenix.* LWT, 1984.

Gilroy, Paul. *The Black Atlantic.* London: Verso, 1993.

Holgate, Dawn. Ed. *Phoenix: Resource/Study Pack.* Leeds: Phoenix Dance, 1997.

hooks, bell. *Yearning: Race, Gender, and Cultural Politics.* Boston: South End Press, 1990.

Mackrell, Judith. "Enough of the B-word." *The Guardian* 21 Apr. 1997: 12–13.

Manning, Susan. "American Document and American Minstrels." *Moving Words.* Ed. Gay Morris. London: Routledge, 1996. 183–202.

Phillips, Mike. *Windrush: A Guide to the Season.* London: BBC, 1998.

—., and Trevor Phillips. *Windrush: The Irresistible Rise of Multi-Racial Britain.* London: HarperCollins, 1998.

Travis, Alan. "Stephen Lawrence's Legacy: Confronting Racist Britain." *The Guardian* 25 Feb. 1999: 1.

An Interview with Isaac Julien

Christy Adair and Ramsay Burt
April 1999, London.

Isaac Julien's contribution to the panel "EmBODYing Liberation" at the 1999 CAAR Conference, "Black Liberation in the Americas," was to talk about his work in general and to show a rough edit of a project he was working on, *Three,* a dance film made with African American choreographers Ralph Lemon and Bebe Miller (See Illus. 6 and 7). This took two forms: a fifteen-minute film and a shorter three-screen video installation. After his session, we asked Julien if we could follow it up with a recorded interview, which took place in April in London. Julien met us at the video editing facility he uses, and he showed us a new version of *Three* incorporating footage they had subsequently shot in New York. This interview is, therefore, about a work which was at the time unfinished, but has subsequently been completed and received its premier in September 1999 at Julien's exhibition at the Victoria Miro Gallery in London. It has also been shown at international film festivals. Some elements of the film that Julien discusses in the interview do not actually appear in the final version – in particular the soundtrack went through a late transformation.

According to Julien, the starting point for *Three* was a live duet, *Two* which Lemon and Miller made and performed in 1986. Having subsequently talked to Miller about the film, we have learnt that this is not strictly true. Lemon and Miller, having not danced together since *Two,* decided in early 1996 to come together to explore some new ideas for a film project. Having initiated this project together, they subsequently approached Julien, who was at the time a visiting professor at the Department of Cinema Studies at New York University. The film gradually took shape over the next three years. Julien chose to introduce a third character into the film, a role played by Cleo Sylvestre, which links *Three* thematically with his earlier film *The Attendant.* Together with Julien's *Trussed,* which also refers to *The Attendant, Three* makes up the final part of a trilogy.

This interview offers insights into Julien's thinking on the politics of representations of the black body and the way that politics has changed and evolved during the 1980s and 90s. Our main interest in approaching Julien was to talk about the relationship between choreography and film making, and in the process Julien provides insights about representation within the creative process.

C.A.   Could we start with discussing ways of working and how the project with Bebe Miller and Ralph Lemon evolved?

I.J.   I was approached by Bebe[Miller] and Ralph [Lemon] when teaching at NYU [New York University], Cinema Studies in 1996. They were interested in me working with them on a dance project. I was interested in working with them because my interest in dance began a long time ago when I studied dance for four years with London Youth Dance Theatre [with Linda Robinson and Hilary Ball from Tower Hamlets School, London]. The project was connected to The Place, a centre for contemporary dance training and events in London from 1976-1986 [Julien joined in 1977]. We studied Graham and Cunningham [dance techniques]. I met Gaby Agis there and she became my pas de deux partner, also Alison Limerick, now a pop star singer – she looks like Judith Jamison. I decided that I did not want to do dance; it is really demanding and needs a specific way of thinking about one's body and movement and I wasn't going to pursue that.

C.A.   So you were working with Gaby before she started her full time training?

I.J.   Yes, she had been dancing for a long time.

C.A.   Yes, she worked with Rosemary Butcher at school.

I.J.   I went to watch a lot of dance at The Place: Rosemary Butcher, London Contemporary Dance Theatre, and Ballet Rambert. This was in the mid to late 1970s.

C.A.   There was a good deal of experimental work at that time at The Place.

I.J.   Yes, and that's where I heard about Yvonne Rainer and Judson. I then went to St. Martin's [School of Art] and after that studied film. Gaby was interested in working with me but that didn't materialize. [Agis says this was a project which became *Freefall*.] Then I began to see work by Sally Potter, and I could see that there was some relationship between dance and film, and some of the early pieces that Agis had done were dances for galleries. I always had that interest in dance. Then my interest dissipated, perhaps because of conservatism in dance. I saw Michael Clarke, Lindsey Kemp and knew people from that company. I was approached by Ralph and Bebe [for this project].

I think Maya Deren's work is amazing. *Study in Choreography for the Camera* and other films she's made have been quite influential in my thinking about space and time and body movement and how in her work all of those things have been transgressed all the time in a sense. Also while teaching at NYU I was very struck by something Annette Michelson [who teaches at NYU] said about silent cinema. This was an idea about the camera being like a fluid, moving object, but with the advent of sound, the technical apparatus including microphones became an increasing burden so that people forgot about the potential for the camera "to dance." It was those sorts of ideas which I was interested in trying to explore with dance, performance and film.

In films like *Looking for Langston* and *Young Soul Rebels* I realize in terms of black cinema, black culture, that within the vernacular song and dance there is precisely the mode of discourse for an exploration of sexuality. It's in Gertrude "Ma" Rainey's songs and "Sissy Blues," sung by George Hanna which we used in *Looking for Langston*, or in some of the work of the trio ,m in the film. There is a dance slightly improvised; the Langston Hughes character and a partner leave together and there is a dance performed by Brothers in Jazz. There was a movement at one time that young black musicians were involved in and Brothers in Jazz used to perform with those musicians.

I am interested in explorations concerned with the body, for example the idea of actors as models, persona-like, an idea which the film director Bresson had that actors are models – one doesn't want the acting one would ordinarily have. There is a freedom linked with the camera, the body, movement. There is something in dance and performance that I want to link that to.

When I look at films produced for *Dance for the Camera* [an ongoing series by the BBC] I never see anything like that happening –possibly because the language for television is so framed and instills a certain sort of vocabulary. At the same time, I realized in the making of this piece that there was a tension. Because originally when I was approached by Bebe and Ralph, they wanted me to film their performance. They were interested in doing a piece of work for film, but the first shooting became a filming of the duet called *Two*. In the filming of the performance and duet which we translated a lot, myself and the photographer, for film, I realized it wasn't translated enough. I wanted to bring it to another position. So the second part of the shooting is choreographed for the camera.

R.B.   Just to check – initially, you started trying to make a good filmed record of existing choreography – then decided to use camera and choreography in a more mutually creative, open-ended way?

I.J.   It was a learning experience for all three of us, but we had to have the basics first, that is the performance, and to understand the piece. Then we went through different processes including workshops, where we were trying to talk about the piece conceptually and what could be brought out in the second stage of filming. I'd seen *Two* on videotape and so had some idea of it.

C.A.   I wondered why they chose *Two* because at that point it was a ten-year-old piece.

I.J.   That's right. I think what was interesting in my discussion with Bebe
          and Ralph was that they were choreographers who had worked in
          companies which were all-white companies, more or less, and that I
          felt quite aligned to their notion of contemporary dance. I understood
          it in relation to their own search for a relationship to modernism and in
          a way to postmodernism which they were thinking about in relation to
          their own practice via race and representation through our collabora-
          tion. Obviously the Alvin Ailey Company and the sort of dance per-
          formed there is not what they are interested in. So where does one find
          the marriage of those sorts of interests?
              Ralph's new work is about ethnicity in some way, marrying it to the
          contemporary aspect, the modern dance aspect. Bebe's new piece is *Up
          Against the Wall*. After their experiences they became interested in
          questions of postcoloniality and became interested in working with me
          because they knew I had been thinking about those sorts of questions.
          My interest is post-identitarian in a way, although not completely. I
          read Homi Bhabha's "The Other Question" in 1983. My Frantz Fanon
          film in 1996 is more like an epilogue for me. Ralph and Bebe were in-
          terested in doing *Two* and coming together as dancers/choreographers
          who don't ordinarily work together but wanted to work together on
          this piece for specific reasons. It is about dystopic and utopic concepts
          of black man/black woman who are thinking about certain sorts of
          questions. The choreographers are interested in certain questions and
          they also come together to meet. The film explores what that dialogue
          is about. With the use of silence and the Cleo Sylvester character, I
          wanted to complicate matters in terms of gender and sexuality, to
          problematize that binary.

C.A.   Yes, that works.

R.B.   Sylvester is the one that gazes. She also has the gaze. At the CAAR
          Conference you mentioned the essay "De Margin and de Centre,"
          which you wrote with Kobena. It raises questions about desire and also
          exploding the binary; so that desire need not necessarily be about black
          desire for white or white for black but about the possibilities of con-
          testation between black voices and black gazes and how mixed race
          problematizes and blurs this. In 1988 you talked about the pleasure at
          being the object of surveillance and about the black man being pun-
          ished within Hollywood narratives for being a source of pleasure –
          parallel to woman being punished in film noir for being a source of
          disruption. I just wondered how those ideas might have related to *Three*
          at all, in terms of theorizing desire?

I.J.   I think a lot of my work has been about a certain visualization of the-
          ory which becomes a model of knowledge in its own right. But now I

feel I want to take a few steps back from that position because after doing the Fanon film there is a way in which that is so embodied in a literalization of that. In *Looking for Langston*, however, it is much more embodied in the way it constructs the visual scene, within the *mis en scene*, the camera movement, the body and how it is placed. That is what I want to go back to. Sometimes there is not always the theoretical language to describe that work. That might be quite good in a way because I think sometimes work needs the space to breathe.

In *Young Soul Rebels* I'm really thinking about those questions a lot: masculinity and the way in which the black subjects are repudiated in narratives for being objects of pleasure, of desire. In *Three* it is much more about the intra-relation of looking via race and gender. In *Looking for Langston* the concern is for what could be seen as a paradigm of the master/slave relation, race relations between black and white, a binary which obviously one wants to trouble. The questions in *Three* are more genderized.

C.A.   In *Looking for Langston* some of the bodies are presented as beautiful objects whereas in *Three* even when Lemon is naked we feel as though the camera cannot contain him. It is more intimate. The couple is intimate, close, not being able to distinguish between each other.

I.J.   There are issues in framing, making them right on the edge of the frame where in certain parts you are not looking completely at the body. The frame is empty. The pastoral scenes intercut between performance-space scenes – like scenes in Maya Deren's films – there is merging, sameness, a matrix building between them

In *The Attendant*, Cleo Sylvestre plays the Conservator character. In *Three* you have her gaze, which is more implicated in the narrative than in *The Attendant*. I wanted *Three* to have a more visceral aspect, for example, the hand touching. There is also something about the narcissism of gay male film-making which I want to problematize a bit with *Three*.

The film looks at the construction of heterosexuality that is somewhat troubled by this other look. Looking – that comes from a response to a text by bell hooks, ["Thinking Through Class: Paying Attention to *The Attendant*"]. The essay on the film talks about the Conservator desiring the phallus but not having the phallus.

Questions about aging and about different types of bodies are important. In *The Attendant*, Thomas Baptiste, who is the museum attendant, is an older black man. Cleo, Bebe and Ralph are also older. In the second stage of filming we chose to shoot using black and white film reversal stock which is not photographic negative but gives harder tonal relations to skin. It doesn't emphasize their age, but it doesn't completely idealize the person. We were considering this way of thinking about it and how to translate this onto the film image itself.

When I showed this to a friend who has worked in film and dance, she didn't like it. The movement in *Two* was done from memory plus improvization. This aspect is meant to be imperfect. The original music was Haitian in the second part and the first part was silent. The aria from Purcell's *Dido and Aeneas* was from *The Attendant*, which was the first film in the trilogy. It draws a correlation between the music and the visual presentation, as this is the last of a trilogy. [Subsequently much of the soundtrack changed.]

C.A.   So will you present it as a trilogy?

I.J.   It might be presented as a trilogy. The fantasies of the Attendant, the white visitor and the Conservator are chronicled in the three films in the trilogy.

R.B.   As we watch the film it has a flow, very much like dance, which has that flow. I was once lucky enough to interview Meredith Monk and she said her model is a musical one, rather than a narrative or a textual model. Dance is always becoming, never fixed. It offers a model of organization through time and space as a flow, as an alternative to mainstream film which is basically text, narrative and character. Maya Deren's work has that sense of flow. Dance almost offers a model of assembling material and a sense of flow through time and space.

I.J.   I find it exciting, almost anti-narrative, which is why it is of interest in my own work. I have made narrative films, but in terms of making experimental films there is a real agency which one has from that way of thinking about movement and the body and the ways desire can be reconfigured within a piece of work. Not rudimentary, linear logic which narrative cinema is prone to use. Sometimes the BBC *Dance for the Camera* films also seem to use this logic.

Javier [de Frutos] and I have an opportunity to work together, but not working for *Dance for the Camera*.

C.A.   So you are working independently?

I.J.   Yes, I am reconstructing some of Javier de Frutos's work as tableaux in another space, working with imagery from the Mexican mariarchi tradition and with "Tex-Mex" images. We are planning to do some filming in San Antonio, Texas, later this year.

R.B.   Will that make more sense for an American audience than a British? I have a sense British audiences don't understand postmodern Latino politics/culture.

I.J.   It's baroque work in that sense, which is drawing from religious idioms that are Catholic. At the same time I am also looking at work connected to ethnicity at its point of origin, where the question of authorship becomes quite interesting in relation to an artist who is non-white or creolized, as Javier is. I do not want to construct an argument which wraps it up too neatly. As well as traditions he has been questioning contemporary discourses, practices.

R.B.   Authorship? People who are not of white dominant discourse? Could you spell it out?

I.J.   There are problems around discussing the work of an artist like Steve McQueen or Chris Ofilli, the Turner Prize winner in 1998. The questions of race and ethnicity become interesting when discussed in relation to an artist who is non-white. There can be a fixing aspect to the way work is discussed aesthetically. For example, when Adrian Searle wrote in the *Guardian* about Ofilli, he used this "black language" to be cool – verbs, descriptive, florid language. Brian Sewell of the *Evening Standard* used another way of writing about the work. He was enchanted by the aesthetic aspect of the work. Authorship becomes slightly shaky in a discussion of aesthetic strategies of work by artists who are non-white in a European context.

Another way of discussing it is to use myself as an example. When I first made experimental film there were questions about why a black filmmaker would make a Godardian film. Why would someone be interested in that sort of exploration that has already been done? There was a conflict between what constitutes the avant-garde and what is the proper place for artists who are non-white. What sort of practices? How should we be recognized?

R.B.   So it is about reception, how work is critically received rather than how work is made? Inevitably artists locate themselves in discourses about what they think they are doing. So, does it affect the artist as well?

I.J.   Yes, it does. For example, artists who proclaim not to be making work about certain questions, when in fact, they are making work about those sorts of questions. Artists will repudiate questions about race and ethnicity in their work so that it can pass into a certain assimilationist sensibility. Other artists take the opposite position that work is supposed to be located in the notion of the black aesthetic – of course, I don't believe that.

C.A.   Has your position on that changed? The notion of a black aesthetic was a popular view in the eighties.

I.J.   I am talking about the repudiation or disavowment of subjects that have been interpolated by a number of different discourses and practices which are both Western and which have a notion of ethnicity or race as part of their make up. Questions concerning people having to be "either/or." That's what I call authorship being on shaky ground. It is a reception question, but it also has an effect. It's a matter of holding both things in place that are important.

The problem with the notion of the black aesthetic, especially when you think about it in relationship to dance, is one of the things Bebe and Ralph are saying in Haitian music or vernacular and rituals. Looking at Maya Deren's films and some other films she shot in Haiti, there is something about the movement which is not just an improvised aspect. They were arguing. Deren was interested in conceiving this to a certain extent.

R.B.   They are suggesting that this is an instance of a black aesthetic within movement traditions?

I.J.   There could be some relationship to that with Maya Deren's interests, which is a sense of ethnography. But for them it was more. There was something that affected them in it. It wasn't just improvised. It wasn't just part of the ritual. It had a structural relationship. A conceptual relationship in terms of movement. The main thing is, if you see the notion of black aesthetic as being somehow out there it means that the business of aesthetics can go on neatly with its own sorts of questions, unaffected by this othering.

That's where you get the problem of language. How do you describe this work? It is interesting to note the responses of the critics looking at work which has black subjects in it or is authored by someone who is black. In a way it's a sort of fiction I think that comes into play.

R.B.   In *Three* there are references to *The Attendant* and to a dominant white aesthetic/culture. In the latter the title role is the black attendant within the museum of white western culture. If you are uneasy with the notion of a black aesthetic, how do artists who are not white situate themselves in relation to a dominant white culture?

I.J.   That's a very interesting question you brought up. It's not the relationship to the dominant culture but questioning, I think, the idea of a claim to that in a pure sort of sense, mediated by some otherness.

The opera and the museum are both paradigmatic locations of western European white dominant culture. By situating the Conservator and the Attendant in these locations, I wanted difference to be placed at the center rather than constructed on the margins. The Conservator's desire is evident in her looking, and there is an attempt to work through some of these ideas but not to visualize theory in the dense, didactic style I developed in *Frantz Fanon, Black Skin White Mask*.

It is really difficult because sometimes if you explain too many things about the work, you literalize what you are trying to do. I have an idea about it; I have my own narrative but that is not necessarily someone else's. As a spectator looking at the piece, it may be completely different. If you (the artist) construct your narrative, that's how it gets read. I don't know how important my narrative is really.

You seem to think it is pretty important. (laughter)

C.A.   Well, it is certainly interesting, but I can see your point of view that you don't want to make too much of it if people then don't go on with their own reading.

I.J.   I see it as the struggle about making work and being in one place and then being in another place, wanting to achieve a certain mobility, fluidity, which gets set back and also the relationship between who is looking. The Conservator looking out gets fixated in that gaze. Going back she's applauding. I see it as the relationship.... I'd better not say it, really. (laughter)

It feels very literal, but I do think there is a way in which one makes art, and then the question of who is looking in the gallery becomes really important. If you make films in the cinema and if they are shown on television, you don't know who is looking; obviously people are. There is the question of demography, audience address, imaging a greater cross section of people.

R.B.   Placing film or video in the form of an installation in an art gallery is quite specific. Part of what the work becomes about is a relationship between the people watching in the gallery and the people on the wall looking back at them. Are the spectators desiring the black dancing bodies they watch? Do they identify with them? That raises problems in relation to identifications across ethnicity.

You may not wish to go too much into your specific interpretation of your work, but it is useful to bring out concepts. It is a question of the way that the scholar relates to the artist. There needs to be a dialogue, and some artists want to know what scholars and critics say about them while others say they don't read the critics.

I.J.   It's been the opposite for me where I have been forced to be a critic of my own work and think about myself. At the time we wrote the essay "De Margin and de Centre" for *Screen* magazine we thought, well, no one will really understand what we are trying to do. And then you have to create a discourse as well, and it's really a lot of work. At that time, we made films, got funding for them and created a theoretical model for discussing work. It is good that doesn't happen any more because it is a burden after awhile.

R.B.   But you needed it.

I.J.   We did.

R.B.   Artists do need a theoretical discourse.

I.J.   Yes, they do need a theoretical discourse, which is why I get annoyed
         with artists who pretend they don't. That's what I call the passing
         game; that's what I am referring to. They do that because they get
         nervous. They think they are going to be fixed. That's what I mean
         about authorship being shaky.

R.B.   Like buck passing, is that what you mean – you can think whatever you
         like.

I.J.   No, passing in terms of race.

C.A.   In the same way, for example, when women artists say, "I'm not a
         woman artist; I'm an artist."

I.J.   Precisely. It is all about the center, universalism, being perceptive and
         making money.

C.A.   So refusing those labels, so that it is possible to pass into the center.

I.J.   Precisely. [In *Three*] the Conservator is a spectator, is the person who
         has the gaze, is looking out to you, you looking, not particularly look-
         ing but trance-like. I have lots of problems about the gallery; I went to
         art school after 1980. I decided not to make work for the gallery; that's
         why I make films. I don't see making work for the gallery as completely
         marvelous. I see it as quite problematic. I see it as recognition of where
         experimental film is: showing work spaces where that work can coexist
         outside of that space is becoming more and more difficult.

Works Cited

Bhabha, Homi K. "The Other Question" *Screen* 24.6 (1983): 18–36.

hooks, bell. "Thinking Through Class: Paying Attention to *The Attendant*." *Reel to
     Real: Race, Sex, and Class at the Movies*. New York : Routledge, 1996. 91–
     96.

Julien, Isaac, and Kobena Mercer. "De Margin and de Centre" *Screen* 29.4 1988:
     2–10.

Filmography

The Attendant (1992) dir. Isaac Julien.

Frantz Fanon, Black Skin White Mask (1996) dir. Isaac Julien.

Freefall (1988) dir. Bob Bentley, choreographed by Gaby Agis.

Looking for Langston (1989) dir. Isaac Julien.

Study in Choreography for the Camera (1945) dir. Maya Deren.

Three (1999) dir. Isaac Julien, choreographed by Ralph Lemon and Bebe Miller.

Trussed (1996) dir. Isaac Julien.

Young Soul Rebels (1991) dir. Isaac Julien.

Afterword

The Shape of Things to Come:
Ruminations on Dancing in a Black Dancing Body

Brenda Dixon Gottschild

I am considered tall – nearly 5 feet 8 inches. Without giving more measure-
ments, let's just say that my torso takes up much less body space than my legs,
with my waist interestingly close to my armpits: short-waisted or stilt-legged
were terms directed at me as a child. In proportion to my legs, my long arms
look fine. Slim hips – none, really – a markedly arched spine, and relatively narrow shoulders complete the picture. Odd? Well, even more extreme contours of
this frame can be seen not only in fashion magazines but also on stages across
the globe in the post-Balanchinian, postmodern era of dance. But that part
comes later. Let me begin in 1957.

As a relatively young dancer (formal studies began when I was 15, but I had
always danced, always wanted to be a dancer), this body got me in trouble.
Shorter, rounder, less muscular, more conventionally proportioned, more
"feminine"dancers were chosen for starring roles in the high school musical or,
later, the dance concerts of the professional dance company that I performed
with by the time I was 19.[1] Certainly, talent, training and discipline may have
figured in artistic decisions to exclude me from those star turns that I lusted
after. But an unspoken, deciding factor was this body which, in the 1950s and
early 1960s, was seen as an anomaly. Still – above and beyond the reality of my
anatomical dimensions – the first and final factor was race: I was a black dancing body housed in chocolate-brown skin, with a head of generously big, nappy
hair, and a full African nose.

By the time I was in my early twenties and making the rounds in the Big
Apple, my friends and I made a point of auditioning for Broadway musicals for
which we knew that even the best African American dancers would not be
hired. But we were young, brash, aspiring dancers. No matter that the dance

---

[1] By the time I was 18 and studying on scholarship at the legendary New Dance Group Studio
in midtown Manhattan, Donya Feuer (now a long time resident of Sweden, where she was
and still is a choreographer and filmmaker), one of my teachers there offered me a
scholarship to come and study with her and her then partner, Paul Sanasardo, at their
Chelsea studio. After a year of daily classes with both of them, I was brought into their
dance company as a sort of supernumerary, along with three other long-limbed dancers
whose body types were nothing like Feuer's, nor her two leading ladies, Chifra Holt and
Milagro Llauger (all of whom were approximately 5 feet 2 inches tall).

establishment thought we were the wrong color or shape (and, of course, like all peoples, we came in many colors and shapes – not only the body "type" described above). It almost didn't matter that we weren't hired (since we were taught that learning to audition and learning to accept rejection was part of sound dance training). We still submitted ourselves to these trials on a regular basis so that our black presence couldn't be totally ignored. Broadway and the American concert dance stage have remained relatively unaffected by Civil Rights advances in other sectors of American life. Yes, there are African American musicals and African American dance companies. But, on the whole, integration does not occur: most American musicals and dance companies are either white or black.[2] How can this situation be justified? Choreographers and directors pull out the old argument that such politicized issues as affirmative action and diversity would restrict their artistic freedom of choice. And, yes, the dance world still likes to think of itself as beyond politics – as though any human system of expression could exist outside that realm.[3]

In 1962 I began to study with Mary Anthony (who had a major effect on my early development as a dancer).[4] Still auditioning, I had a strange experience with dancer/choreographer Pearl Lang. I responded to her call, not for a featured role, but to work as a pick-up in a small chorus of four dancers. I was informed, after auditioning, that it wasn't a matter of race (the concept of *racism* wasn't even considered), but I could not be used because my skin color would

---

[2] A typical example was *Swing!*, the dance-based Broadway hit of year 2000, that had a token black in the cast: an irony, since swing originated in the African American community in the 1920s and 1930s and was regarded as a black form until white practitioners (like Benny Goodman and the Dorsey Brothers) jumped on the bandwagon and disseminated the form to the white mainstream populace.
     Reviewing Berlin, Germany's 1999 "Tanz Im August" Festival for *Dance Magazine*, (November 1999, 83-85) I observed a degree of ethnic diversity within European dance companies that underscores its absence in the United States of America. Ensembles based in Munich (Rui Horta Stage Works), Prague (Deja Donne) and Brussels (Rosas) all included a wider diversity of peoples of color than the postmodern "white" dance groups in a city like Philadelphia, where I now reside.

[3] In this regard I must mention a comment made by Steve Paxton, father of the contact improvisation movement, in the Dance in America film, *Beyond the Mainstream* (directed by Merrill Brockway, New York: WNET-TV, 1980). He talks about the contact improviser's state of mind as receptive, open, and, to use his word, "apolitical."

[4] Indeed, my time with Anthony coincided with the Civil Rights era. I remember when she was offered a booking at the Virginia Fine Arts Museum in Richmond. Such places were still segregated (ca. 1964-5). She made it a point to inform that institution that she wouldn't perform there unless she was allowed to have an integrated company. Soon after, she invited me to perform with her ensemble. We played in Richmond and may very well have been the first integrated group to perform there. (Of course, integration meant that I was the sole member of color in this small ensemble, and that the audience was still segregated. But Anthony's voice was heard, and her/our point was made.)

"destroy the unity of the corps," a phrase that still sticks in my craw. Lang was reacting to my skin color. I guess if I could have "passed," it wouldn't have mattered. I don't really know. Elsewhere I have written about this incident[5]: it struck me as ironic and frustrating that dancers could live in fantasy worlds, wear tutus, be Wilis or princesses, goddesses or witches, but black skin in a dance based on some Greek tragic theme (Lang still choreographed in the manner of her mentor, Martha Graham) would be destructive to some principle of unity.

So there I was, early on, aware of the barriers and boundaries that the black dancing body represented to the white dance hierarchy. But, even then, in the 1950s and 1960s, I saw ample evidence to show that those same qualities that were repulsed were also desired. Why else would black forms of music and dance which took their shape, rhythm, accent – color, if you will – from black initiatives be the reigning soul and spirit in American culture? Why else would Elvis Presley imitate, to the letter, the sound of Big Mama Thornton, an African American rhythm and blues singer, to create his early hit, "You Ain't Nothin But a Hound Dog," and then go on the Ed Sullivan Show dancing (or, as the press of the era would say, "gyrating his pelvis") as though he were the white answer to Jackie Wilson? Closer to my dance home, why else would the revered George Balanchine have used the markers of African American dance to create *The Four Temperaments* (1946), *Agon* (1957), *Jewels* (1967), and a host of other modern ballet masterpieces?[6] And why would modern dancers turn to bare feet, use of the floor, grounded energy, and articulation of the torso – elements that were Africanist in nature – as basic components in their revisionist strategy?

WHY WAS IT THAT THE WHITE WORLD LOVED THE CULTURE BUT DESPISED ITS CREATORS – LOVED THE BLACK DANCE BUT HATED THE BLACK DANCER?

The only answer I have found to this question is the ongoing power of racism and its perpetual grip on world consciousness (and we can no longer assume that anti-black racism is unique to any one nation). The irony, here, is that racism is rearing its head in new and more complex ways at the same time that theories of race are facing extinction by the world of academic scholarship. For example, on careful investigation and cross-cultural comparisons, theories of body types that exist according to racial profiling have been proven to be scientifically unsound. There is enough variation *within* any ethnic group to make the theory worthless. Likewise, there are enough examples of other body types *across*

---

5   See Dixon Gottschild, Brenda. "Black Dance and Dancers and the White Public: A Prolegomenon to Problems of Definition." *Black American Literature Forum.* Spring 1990, 117–23.

6   For a full treatment of Africanisms in Balanchine and throughout white American culture, see Dixon Gottschild, *Digging the Africanist Presence in American Performance: Dance and Other Contexts* (Greenwood 1996, 1998).

ethnic groups to further debunk any ethnic body type theory. Why? Because there are no "pure" ethnic types – no races, as such. Europeans, Africans, Asians – we are all mixed bloods, mixed "races."[7] All evidence points to the fact that race is not a biological imperative, but a social construct (convenient for purposes of classification and differentiation).

In spite of scientific findings, many people still buy into the old ways of thinking. On the one hand some African Americans, proud to be who they are and sick and tired of racial oppression, ascribe to the old racial science but *revise the canon* and use those categories to affirm that black is beautiful. For example, an African American doctoral candidate at Harvard University (whom I met at the August, 2000 City Center Katherine Dunham Institute, where I was a guest faculty member), stated that she was upset by the new thinking about race: she is black, Others are not, and that means something positive, not negative. From her perspective, as soon as blacks became ready to constructively utilize the idea of separate races, white scholars decided that race was outdated. On the other hand, white dance critic Joan Acocella, in a review of the Alvin Ailey company in *The New Yorker* (27 Dec. and 3 Jan., 2000, 138–141), praises the Ailey (black) dancers to high heaven, after dismissing Ailey's choreography as second rate. Near the end, she asserts that "In my experience, black dancers, on average, are better than white dancers" (141), then coyly inserts the "nature or nurture" question as an afterthought. Both claims give renewed credence and fresh energy to the old race theories. Well, so much for new approaches to writing dance criticism.

BUT IF WE LET GO OF THE CONCEPT OF RACE, WHERE WOULD WE HANG OUR RACISM?

And therein lies the tale. Here we are, with a foot in the twenty-first century, still talking about black dance, black dancers, and the black dancing body! What are we really talking about? A phantom? A prejudice? A stereotype? An ideal? A limitation? And if we speak of a black dancing body, then is there also a white dancing body, an Asian dancing body, and so on? How and what differentiates these separate bodies? Who is studying them? Where? And to what end? How is the information being gathered? Because of the persistence of global racism we are stuck with talking about a social construct in jejeune biological terms. But that dilemma is a righteous indication of who we are and where we are, as people on this earth at this point in time: entrenched in the thrall of our own skewed constructs. We inherit the language we deserve, and that language shapes our perceptions.

What I find amazing about this predicament is how the paradigm of the black dancing body has shifted, over the course of the twentieth century, into

---

[7] Although this reductive explanation of race theory is rough and rudimentary, it does adhere to state-of-the-art research.

mainstream white acceptability. Although the black dancer remains the Other, the black body has, through dance, sports, fashion, and everyday lifestyle, become the last word in white desirability. Going back to my description of my own body, those characteristics – long limbs, short torso, arched spine, narrow hips and shoulders – scream out at us from print, video, and film media and from stages and sports arenas across the globe. And just look how this mythical quotient has changed the shape of the ballet body. As Arthur Mitchell – founder and artistic director of the Dance Theater of Harlem – pointed out, George Balanchine "described his ideal ballerina as having a short torso, long arms, long legs, and a small head. If that's ideal, then we [black folk] are perfect."[8] No wonder the Harvard graduate student wants to stake her claim! And me, too: finally my awkward goose is the graceful swan – the black body no longer the black sheep; the black swan preempting the white one! All joking aside, the black dancing body (and, yes, we are stuck with the phrase) is, was, and has been the shape of things to come – both loved and despised – in the minstrel, vaudeville, jazz, swing, and rock-funk-soul eras of the two preceding centuries.

At the modern/postmodern crossroads, when the times were mightily a-changin', the gifted composer/musician Ornette Coleman was carrying out his own revolutionary civil rights era in sound. He released an album called *Tomorrow Is the Question!* followed by another titled *The Shape of Jazz To Come*. Like its musical counterparts, the black dancing body was the stamp and shape of twentieth century modernism and postmodernism. For now – with a foot in the twenty-first century and African American-based hip hop culture a global phenomenon – can we bet on that body to continue as the shape of things to come?

Brenda Dixon Gottschild
Philadelphia, November 2000

---

8   "Talk of the Town." *The New Yorker* 28 Dec. 1987: 36.

Contributors

Christy Adair is a dance historian and facilitator, contributing articles and reviews to journals, magazines, and radio. She is the author of *Women and Dance: Sylphs and Sirens* (Macmillan 1992). She also teaches dance studies at the University of Hull and the Northern School of Contemporary Dance and is currently researching archival histories for Phoenix Dance.

Michael Borshuk is currently completing his doctoral studies in English at the University of Alberta. His research analyses the political and aesthetic influence of jazz on African American modernist literature. He also writes on jazz for CODA magazine.

Ramsay Burt is Senior Research Fellow in Dance at De Monfort University in the United Kingdom. His *The Male Dancer* (Routledge 1995) focuses on representations of masculinity in British new dance. His book *Alien Bodies: Representations of Modernity, "Race" and Nation in Early Modern Dance* was published by Routledge in 1998. In 1999 he was visiting professor at the Department of Performance Studies, New York University.

Thomas F. DeFrantz is Assistant Professor of Theater Arts at the Massachusetts Institute of Technology and directs the dance history program at the Alvin Ailey School of American Dance. He is author of the forthcoming *Revelations: Alvin Ailey's Embodiment of African American Culture*. He has published widely on the black body in concert dance, dance in the Black Arts movement, and hip hop dance.

Brenda Dixon Gottschild was Professor of Dance Studies at Temple University for over 15 years. She writes for *Dance Magazine* and is the author of *Digging the Africanist Presence in American Performance: Dance and Other Contexts* (Greenwood Press 1996 and 1998) and *Waltzing in the Dark: African American Vaudeville and Race Politics in the Swing Era* (St. Martin's Press 2000). Her *Afterword* in this collection touches on topics that she explores in her forthcoming book, *The Black Dancing Body – A Geography From Coon to Cool* (St. Martin's Press).

Dorothea Fischer-Hornung is senior lecturer in the English Department at Ruprecht-Karls-Universität Heidelberg, Germany. Among her publications are *Women in the United States* (Bayerischer SchulBuchVerlag 1990); *Women and War* (Berg 1991), with Maria Diedrich; and *Holding Their Own: Perspectives on the Multi-Ethnic Literatures of the United States* (Stauffenburg Verlag 2000), with Heike

Raphael-Hernandez. Her interest currently focuses on Katherine Dunham's career in Europe

Alison D. Goeller teaches literature and writing for the University of Maryland, European Division in Heidelberg, Germany. She has published articles on Eudora Welty, the American poet H.D. and most recently the novelist Tina De Rosa in the volume *Holding Their Own: Perspectives on the Multi-Ethnic Literatures of the United States.* She studied ballet and modern dance for over 25 years in both the U.S. and England.

Dorota Janowska graduated from Maria Curie-Sklodowska University in Lublin, Poland, where she majored in American Literature. She has presented papers both in Poland and other European countries on various aspects of African American dance. Currently, she is a junior Fulbright scholar at Temple University, working towards a Ph.D. in dance history.

Isaac Julien is an English film maker who is firmly established in the vanguard of the Independent British Cinema. Co-founder of the film and video workshop *Sankofa,* he first gained international recognition with his controversial film meditation of the life and poetry of Langston Hughes, *Looking for Langston* (1989), and the feature film *Young Soul Rebels* (1991). He has served on the editorial board of *Screen* magazine and been a visiting professor at New York University and Harvard University.

Anthea Kraut is a doctoral student in the Theatre and Drama Program at Northwestern University. Her work on Zora Neale Hurston's staging of black vernacular dance has been published in *Theatre Studies.* She is the recipient of Second Prize, The Society of Dance History Scholars' 1999 Selma Jeanne Cohen Young Scholars Award Program and a 1999 Graduate Research Award from CORD (Congress on Research in Dance).

Wendy Perron was a member of the Trisha Brown Company from 1975 to 1978, the first choreographer from the U.S. to win a DAAD fellowship to Berlin in 1992, and one of eight subjects in the Michael Blackwood documentary, *Retracing Steps: American Dance Since Postmodernism.* A former associate director of Jacob Pillow's Dance Festival, she has taught dance technique, composition, improvisation, criticism, and history at Bennington College, Princeton University, SUNY Purchase, Rutgers University, New York University, Mt. Holyoke, and the Trisha Brown studio. She is currently the New York Editor of *Dance Magazine.*